NEW TESTAMENT MESSAGE

A Biblical-Theological Commentary
Wilfrid Harrington, O.P. and Donald Senior, C.P.
EDITORS

New Testament Message, Volume 21

THE JOHANNINE EPISTLES

Pheme Perkins

 Michael Glazier, Inc.
Wilmington, Delaware

ABOUT THE AUTHOR

Pheme Perkins is on the faculty of Boston College. She holds a Ph.D. in New Testament and Christian Origins from Harvard University, is a member of the editorial boards of the *Catholic Biblical Quarterly* and the *Journal of Biblical Literature*. Among her many publications are *The Gospel According to John*; *Hearing the Parables of Jesus* and *The Gnostic Dialogue*.

Revised edition 1984

Michael Glazier, Inc.
1723 Delaware Avenue
Wilmington, Delaware 19806

First printing 1979

The Bible text in this publication is from the Revised Standard Version of the Bible, copyrighted in 1946, 1952 © 1971, 1973 by the Division of Christian Education of the National Council of the Churches of Christ in the U.S.A., and used by permission.

Library of Congress Catalog Card Number: 79-55808
International Standard Book Number:
    New Testament Message series: 0-89453-123-9
    JOHANNINE EPISTLES: 0-89453-144-1

Printed in the United States of America

Contents

EDITORS' PREFACE

New Testament Message is a commentary series designed to bring the best of biblical scholarship to a wide audience. Anyone who is sensitive to the mood of the church today is aware of a deep craving for the Word of God. This interest in reading and praying the Scriptures is not confined to a religious elite. The desire to strengthen one's faith and to mature in prayer has brought Christians of all types and all ages to discover the beauty of the biblical message. Our age has also been heir to an avalanche of biblical scholarship. Recent archaeological finds, new manuscript evidence, and the increasing volume of specialized studies on the Bible have made possible a much more profound penetration of the biblical message. But the flood of information and its technical nature keeps much of this scholarship out of the hands of the Christian who is eager to learn but is not a specialist. *New Testament Message* is a response to this need.

The subtitle of the series is significant: "A Biblical-Theological Commentary." Each volume in the series, while drawing on up-to-date scholarship, concentrates on bringing to the fore in understandable terms the specific message of each biblical author. The essay-format (rather than a word-by-word commentary) helps the reader savor the beauty and power of the biblical message and, at the same time, understand the sensitive task of responsible biblical interpretation.

A distinctive feature of the series is the amount of space given to the "neglected" New Testament writings, such as Colossians, James, Jude, the Pastoral Letters, the Letters of Peter and John. These briefer biblical books make a significant but often overlooked contribution to the richness of the New Testament. By assigning larger than normal coverage to these books, the series hopes to give these parts of Scripture the attention they deserve.

Because *New Testament Message* is aimed at the entire English speaking world, it is a collaborative effort of international proportions. The twenty-two contributors represent biblical scholarship in North America, Ireland, Britain and Australia. Each of the contributors is a recognized expert in his or her field, has published widely, and has been chosen because of a proven ability to communicate at a popular level. And, while all of the contributors are Roman Catholic, their work is addressed to the Christian community as a whole. The New Testament is the patrimony of all Christians. It is the hope of all concerned with this series that it will bring a fuller appreciation of God's saving Word to his people.

Wilfrid Harrington, O.P.
Donald Senior, C.P.

PREFACE

BECAUSE WE DID NOT WANT to burden the readers of this series with the weight of scholarly debate, many of those to whom I am indebted for my understanding of the Johannine writings will remain anonymous, hidden behind the "some scholars say" and like expressions. The suggested readings at the end will indicate who some of them are, and I trust that the more learned reader will have no difficulty attaching names to the various strands of Johannine scholarship reflected in these pages. I owe a particular debt of gratitude to Donald Senior, one of the editors of the series, who suggested I write this book. Though I have worked on the fourth gospel for some years, it had not occurred to me to try unravelling the perplexities of the Johannine letters. The experience of doing so has proven both more fruitful and more interesting than I might have predicted at the outset. And I trust that the reader will also find more here than his or her initial expectations of such unimposing writings might suggest.

In the five years since the first ediction of this commentary, New Testament scholars have continued to find sociological and anthropological models helpful in describing what it meant to live as a Christian in the first and second centuries. We have seen increased emphasis on the role of rituals and symbols in creating the self-identity of Christians and the importance of a community's ability to define itself in terms of its description of the larger world. Many studies have also attempted to understand the nature of authority in early Christian communities and the peculiar polemics of the Johannine writings. In addition, Raymond

Brown has published a commentary many times longer than this one on the Johannine epistles. Therefore, it seemed best to take the occasion of a new printing to undertake a complete revision of the commentary in this series rather than to leave it with minor modifications. What remains the same does so because, despite some harsh criticism from Prof. Brown, it still seems to me to represent the best way of understanding the situation out of which the epistles are written.

Finally, the problem of sexist language in the Johannine epistles must be addressed. Feminist theologians and exegetes have rightly insisted that the New Testament often uses masculine words in reference to Christian communities even when it presupposes that those communities included both men and women (see E. Fiorenza, *In Memory of Her*, 45f). For a community which preserved such rich traditions about the role of women (see the discussion in R. Brown, *Community of the Beloved Disciple*, 183-98), the concentration of masculine references in the epistles comes as something of a shock.

Elsewhere in christianity the love command is phrased as "loving one's neighbor"; in the fourth gospel as "loving one another," an expression which also occurs in the letters. "Brother" as the designation for christians only appears twice in the gospel: in the risen Jesus' command to Mary (20:17) where it refers to Peter and the disciples, and in the account of the beloved disciple's death (21:23), a passage written by a disciple of the evangelist, perhaps even the author of the Johannine letters. In the letters, the situation is quite different. Not only is "brothers" a standard way to refer to christians (1 Jn 3:13; 5:16; 3 Jn 3,5,10); it is employed in many of the formulations of the love command (1 Jn 2:9.10,11; 3:10,14,15,16,17; 4:20,21). Contrast this situation with the ethical exhortation in Jas 2:14-16, for example. Though that author addresses his audience as "brothers," the deeds by which they show their faith are helping a "brother or sister" in need. 1 Jn 2:12-14 ties the more general Johannine self-designation "children" together with "fathers" and "young men."

We suspect that this preference for "brothers" is no accident but derives from the fact that the parties involved in the disputes which occasioned these writings were men. Both the false teachers and the author's missionary associates are "brethren." Contrast that situation with the condemnation of a woman as a false prophet and teacher in Rev 2:10-23. Undoubtedly the paraenetic tradition on which the author drew to remind his audience of what they had heard "from the beginning" had been addressed to both men and women. But the author clearly conceives his audience as men. Male missionaries, leaders and teachers are the ones involved in thrashing out the problems about which these letters are speaking. Therefore, we will attempt to retain the masculine references when they appear to refer to opponents conceived as men with whom the author is in dispute and to use the more inclusive language of "brothers and sisters" for traditional paraenesis. We have no way of knowing the extent to which, if not at all, women were involved in these disputes. Since the opponents have formed an alternate community, that community must have included both men and women from the original Johannine circles.

INTRODUCTION

Why Read the Johannine Letters?

WHEN ASKED what is the New Testament, most people can come up with the gospels, maybe Acts, the major Pauline letters, maybe Hebrews and Revelation, but the ten smaller letters, of which 1-3 John are a distinct group, are almost never mentioned. The few who do mention them usually have no idea what they are about. Though not as theologically exciting as the major New Testament writings, these letters do have a fascination of their own. They let us into the world of early christian communities struggling to establish themselves as part of the larger graeco-roman world. We always need to be reminded of how very small christianity was during its first century. Many christian claims reveal their astonishing, even revolutionary, character only when we get beyond our picture of christianity, the world religion, back to the "grass roots" origins of the movement. It is just those "grass roots" that we recover when we read the small, less known writings in the New Testament like the Johannine letters.

However, we hasten to add that the "grass roots" are not without their own insights and genuine developments of christian spirit and understanding. For example, "God is love," a statement many would regard as the greatest insight and foundation of devotional christianity, appears here in 1 Jn 4; not in the gospels or letters of Paul—though there is much in their universally shared conviction of God's unremitting care for his creation to found such a conclusion. 1 Jn also insists that a person must believe in Jesus, a flesh and blood person, as revelation of God's love and must belong to the community which is to embody that love, if one is to be saved. Most christians would agree that his convictions represent ideals of christian belief and practice. In 1 Jn, we have the opportunity to see how these ideals came to be expressed in a concrete situation; how they were understood to be at the foundation of christian community. Then we can enter into our own dialogue with the author: how do his insights challenge contemporary christian reflection?

The Authorship and Context of the Johannine Letters

Since these writings are traditionally referred to as 1-3 John, one might assume that they are by the author of the Gospel of John. But, if you read them through quickly, you will see that they never make such a claim for themselves. The author is only claiming the authority of a teacher who knows what the testimony to Jesus "from the beginning" has been. He never appeals to what he has written before. (Unlike Luke at the beginning of Acts or Paul in 2 Cor, for example.) Yet we cannot say that the letters were written before the gospel. Look carefully through the Gospel of John and you will see that it focuses on problems created for the community by jewish opponents, who have expelled christians from the synagogue communities (Jn 16:1-4a). They are insisting that it is blasphemous to speak of Jesus as Son of the Father (see the debate in Jn 8). The Johannine letters, on the other hand, describe problems of internal strife, not external persecution. No one is denying the divinity of Jesus; but some christians are accused of denying his coming "in the flesh" (see 1 Jn 4:2). Judaism is not mentioned. 1 Jn 5:21 warns christians to beware of idols. The majority of the community would now seem to be pagan converts rather than former jews.

But, if the letters are not by the author of the gospel, (see Brown, *Epistles of John*, 14-35, for a thorough discussion of authorship and sequence of the gospel and epistles), then the author must still have been close to the evangelist. 1 Jn uses many symbols and expressions from his work. Since many interpreters of the gospel think that a disciple gave it its final form after the evangelist had died—adding some of the latter's preaching and explaining his death—this disciple might even have been the author of the letters. Part of the change in focus between the gospel and the letters shows that christians now have to articulate for themselves what they believe. They are not responding to the external pressures and arguments of jews or jewish christians as in the gospel. Most interpreters agree that even the views opposed by the author of 1-2 Jn were developed as interpretations of the fourth gospel's picture of Jesus. But these views were not merely theological speculation for its own sake, they were creating serious problems for the community. Relationships between christians have become strained (2-3 Jn). Many scholars like to think of 1 Jn as the first commentary on, perhaps even better, the first pastoral application of the gospel.

Because he is writing to a specific group of communities, "churches," all of which belong to the Johannine tradition, the author leaves us with many questions. He does not need to explain in detail the views he is opposing. He can just allude to them or perhaps, parody some of his opponents' favorite expressions. There are also passages in 1 Jn which look as though they are independent sections. Perhaps they are examples of the kind of paraenesis, (ethical exhortation), that was frequently used in Johannine churches. The author can then make his case for true christian tradition by referring to them. We can sometimes guess that a passage derives from such traditional preaching, when we find that its form or content is like christian preaching from nonjohannine traditions found in other parts of the New Testament or in early christian writings. We will be asking you to look at such passages elsewhere in the New Testament as we go along. But often, we find ourselves in the position of having to guess what the opponents might have been saying, and sometimes the information given is not sufficient for us to be sure.

Three kinds of external evidence can also help us to understand the Johannine communities better. First, thanks to archaeology, the study of ancient inscriptions, and the thousands of private and public letters, documents, and writings that have survived on papyri in Egypt, historians know more and more about how people lived and related to one another at this time. They also help clarify our picture of the religious ideas held and the religious associations formed by inhabitants of the cities of the eastern part of the empire. Thus, we have a better picture of what people expected of each other and their gods.

Secondly, the Dead Sea Scrolls, writings of the jewish Essenes found at Qumran, continue to yield a wealth of information about the organization, beliefs and practices of a first century jewish community. Although there is no evidence to support the claim that christianity derived from the essene sect, their writings have shown us examples of scriptural interpretation, community organization, and theological language about God, humanity and the impending end of the world, which illuminate many facets of the New Testament. These comparisons suggest that the Scrolls and the New Testament traditions independently reflect religious beliefs and practices common across a broad spectrum of 1st century judaism. Even when the Gospel of John was written, sometime around A.D. 90, christians found their exclusion from the wider jewish community painful. Some people may even have preferred to remain jewish rather than to publicly admit their belief in Jesus as messiah (cf. Jn 12:42f). We may assume, then, that the parallels to essene language and perhaps community rule became part of the tradition of the Johannine community during its period of close association with judaism. They form part of the past tradition which the author wants his audience to recall as he assesses new claims about Jesus and christian salvation. We will see that he takes a similar stance toward some traditional christian formulae.

Although written later than the Johannine letters, newly published gnostic writings from Nag Hammadi (in Egypt) can help us understand some of the ideas the opponents seem to have been trying out. Comparisons between 1 Jn and patristic accounts of the gnostics had long ago suggested to people that the author's opponents might have been christians whose theology had taken a gnostic turn. They are clearly not gnostics in the sense of the 2nd century christian gnostics. There is not even the slightest hint that they would deny that the Father of Jesus and the creator god are one and the same, as 2nd century gnostics regularly do. Nor, as far as we can tell, have the opponents carried speculation about the nature of Jesus as revealer to the lengths that 2nd century gnostic interpreters of the fourth gospel would do. But the piety of these opponents and their rejection of a sacrificial interpretation of the death of Jesus certainly find a home in later gnostic tradition. The new writings give us examples of the gnostics' explanations of Jesus, their ideal of community, and their own polemic against orthodox christianity. They help us correct many false ideas about gnosticism which are still being used to interpret statements in the Johannine writings, and the traditions reflected in the christian gnostic writings themselves provide further clues as to what these opponents might have been saying.

Finally, we would agree with many interpreters who point out that the problems reflected in the Johannine letters are a microcosm of the process any religious community must go through as it tries to consolidate what it has gained from the past—its teaching, its ritual, its image of the founder, its ideal of community—in the face of the future and the changing socio-religious context of its members. It must find new interpretations of that past and new forms of internal organization.

Literary Characteristics of the Letters

Although we commonly refer to all three writings as "letters," they represent three different literary genres. 1 Jn is not a letter at all, but an instructional tract which may have been intended to be circulated among several communities. 2 Jn is a letter to a community or group of communities which are different from that in which the author usually lives, but close enough for him to suggest that he may visit them. 3 Jn is a private letter to a friend, Gaius, who lives in yet another community. Both 2 & 3 Jn are like the private letters that survive on papyrus, but also have features in common with the christian letter form as we know it from the Pauline correspondence.

Before turning to the individual writings, a brief description of the author's method of composition may help you read them. See how many examples of the various features you can come up with yourself.

Some scholars have attempted to isolate a written source, which the author then rewrote in composing 1 Jn. However, there does not seem to be enough stylistic and linguistic evidence to support reconstruction of such an independent source. We shall also argue that such a method of sticking together texts is unlike the author's tendency toward allusion and oral composition. Instead of supposing that the author has revised some text, we think that he has a variety of sources at his disposal, most of them oral in character. He appeals to a number of traditional formulae. Some of them derive from christian tradition older than the fourth gospel. The fourth gospel, itself, seems to draw on synoptic-like traditions about Jesus, which may have circulated freely in the Johannine church. Other allusions to synoptic-like tradition in 1 Jn probably derive from the same source (cp. for example, 1 Jn 3:7//Mk 13:5, and Mt 5:48; 1 Jn 5:3//Mt 11:30). The author treats the fourth gospel in the same fashion. He does not quote it as we would but alludes to it. (1 Jn 1:4=Jn 15:11; 1 Jn 3:11=Jn 15:12 come closer to being direct quotations, but they may have been used as formulae in the community.) Some of the slogans the author uses to distinguish true christian belief from false seem to have been formulated during the controversy with the jews at the time the gospel was written. Confession that "Jesus is messiah (christ)" or "son of God" was a badge of christian allegiance and willingness to suffer persecution. 1 Jn is using the old slogan in a new situation where christians are divided among themselves. Jewish accusations against christian belief are no longer an issue; he does not appeal to the Old Testament. (Brown, *Epistles*, 291f, suggests that the author may have imitated the gospel's use of Isa 6:10 in Jn 12:39-40 to speak of the blindness of his opponents. In that case, 1 Jn depends upon the gospel's tradition rather than on the OT itself.)

Most exegetes agree that 1 Jn presumes its readers are familiar with the Johannine tradition as reflected in the gospel. Since those whom the author opposes also claim to stand in the Johannine tradition, 1 Jn can be viewed as calling the community to witness to the author's understanding as the correct interpretation of the gospel. Yet, 1 Jn does not contain direct quotations from the Fourth Gospel as we know it. Rather, the allusions appear to lie slightly below the surface. The opening prologue (1 Jn 1:1-5) speaks of a revelation of life, light, what is in the presence of God and creation of a communion between the believer and the Father through the Son in a way that reminds the reader of the opening of the gospel (Jn 1:1-18; see the extensive charts in Brown, *Epistles*, 176-80). Perhaps, the structure of 1 Jn has also been shaped by the gospel's division into a "Book of Signs" about Jesus' public ministry and a "Book of Glory," Jesus' revelation of himself and the love command to believers. [So Brown, *Epistles*, 124-27, who divides 1 Jn into Part One (1:5-3:10), the gospel, that God is light, obligates the believer to walk in light, and Part Two (3:11-5:12), the love command obligates believers to love one another].

1 & 2 Jn use the same polemic categories to describe their opponents within the Johannine community as the gospel had used for outsiders, "the Jews" or "the world." It would appear that the Johannine tradition provided a set of dualistic categories, such as light/darkness; of God/of the devil; truth/falsehood, that could be applied in any situation. Thus, we see that the language of the epistles is often highly tradition. They embody a rhetorical tradition that has been shaped in the earlier experiences of the community. When

we read the epistles, we need to constantly ask ourselves whether or not we can take such traditional language as an accurate representation of the new situation confronting the community.

Other examples of the rhetorical art of the Johannine community occur in the patterned repetitions of clauses and themes. Earlier commentators often hoped to detect written sources used by the author of 1 Jn in these patterns. For example, 1 Jn constructs sentences that are formulaic parallels using conditional clauses, "if x ... ", or, the definite article plus a participle, "everyone who does x ... " (1 Jn 1:6,8,10; 2:4,6,9). Another favorite device is antithetic parallelism, stating the same thing positively and then negatively (4:7f). Or, we find use of genuine antitheses (1 Jn 3:7-10; 4:4-6; 5:18f; 3 Jn 11) in constructing a passage. Word associations help link one section to another. Then end of a section may return to a word or words from its beginning. It is such rhetorical structures and associative links between words and images from one section to the next that provide the forward movement of the epistles. The author does not provide us with an argument set out in logical sequence to be analyzed but one which is to be heard, which turns on spiral, thematic associations. Such forms of speech do not permit us to conclude that every variation implies that a different problem or opinion is being attacked. Indeed, they make it difficult for us to reconstruct the opponents' position from the author's argument against it.

Division and Authority in the Johannine Community

Studies of the disputes between Christians in Paul's letters to the Corinthians have suggested that some of the tensions were created by Christians who assembled in different households. No single house was likely to have held the number of people in the Christian community of Corinth. Different groups developed different solutions to theological problems, different perspectives on salvation, and even some rivalry in their allegiance to different apostles. Even though Paul and his associates founded the Corinthian church, Paul finds it difficult to establish unity among the various factions there. This model of the church in a given city as a collection of household groups appears to be the fundamental pattern of community life in the churches of the hellenistic mission generally and is not unique to Paul. Jn 4:53 preserves a formula from the tradition when we are told that the royal official "believed and all his household with him." (see Meeks, *Urban Christians*, 74-84). Early Christian communities were small, face-to-face groups in which a high degree of interaction between all members of the group is possible. This small-group character is also reflected in the frequent advice to Christians to admonish and support one another. At the same time, traveling Christians regularly received and expected hospitality from groups in other cities (*Urban Christians*: 109).

Although Pauline and Petrine communities appear to have developed specific church offices to replace the authority that Paul, for example, exercises over the churches of his mission (Tim 1:9; 1 Tim 5:17), the Johannine epistles lack such a development. They continue to insist upon the mutual discernment and correction within the community, which is grounded in a perception of the church as "spirit-endowed," a phrase often used of Paul's understanding of community (1 Jn 2:20,27). The fourth gospel had insisted that the Paraclete, the Holy Spirit, would follow Jesus as witness to the truth and serve to guide the community (Jn 14:15-16; 15:26-27; 16:3). The difficulties of this situation emerge in the dispute reflected in the epistles. The author cannot appeal to any authority to decide whether his understanding of the tradition or that of his opponents is correct. He must refer to the guidance of the Spirit, even though he knows that his opponents will do likewise. The community must be brought to reject "that spirit" (1 Jn 4:1). He speaks of the witnesses to the tradition handed down within the community itself, evoked with the "we" in 1 Jn 1:5. These witnesses would have included the Beloved Disciple, the evangelist, and other disciples of the Beloved Disciple including the author of the epistles. Some scholars have described this group of witnesses as a "Johannine school." However, it does not function according to the authoritative model of teacher/students typical of the ancient schools. No one inherited the mantle of the Beloved Disciple or of the evangelist as head of the group. Therefore, Brown suggests that we think of it as a community of witnesses (*Epistles*: 94-96; Brown thinks that the author calls himself "presbyter" in 2 & 3 Jn as one who had received the tradition from the eye-witness generation but that he does not use this appelation in 1 Jn because he is deliberately assuming the mantle of the evangelist.)

The sociological pattern of the Johannine communities helps us understand the ease with which Christians could become divided over the truth of the same tradition. The intensity of emotion that we find in the epistles could also be understood on the basis of such small group dynamics. In addition, the Johannine community appears to have become even more closely knit than many churhes through its experience of persecution. The gospel attests that hostility from Jewish authorities had cost community members (e.g. Jn 9:22, 34c). Jewish persecution may have been followed by hostility from the gentile environment into which the community and its mission moved (Jn 16:1-4a; 15:18). The Johannine churches identified their fate as "hated" with the hatred shown Jesus by a hostile world. It was a badge of true discipleship. Along with this understanding of its suffering, the community developed an intense feeling of its inner unity, of the mutual love of Christians, and of the presence of the Father, Son, Spirit to the community (Jn 15:24-27; 17:9-23).

Exploration of the use of the expession *koinonia* (fellowship) in the Pauline mission suggests additional factors in the breakdown of community that we find in the Johannine epistles (see Perkins, "Koinonia"). The author's opponents also claim to have *koinonia* and the following among Christians from the Johannine churches to support that claim (1 Jn 1:6; 4:5). The Johannine understanding of the unity between members of the community and with God expressed in terms such as "remain in" or "be in" God (1 Jn

1:3, 6) invests *koinonia* with a theological richness typical of the Johannine tradition. However, the expression is not typical of that tradition. In the Pauline writings, it belongs to a cluster of terms which describe the association of Christians and the apostle for the purpose of sharing the gospel with others. Such associations, in legal terms, were regularly described as requiring unanimity of purpose, mutual regard, concern for the interests of the partnership rather than one's own interests. This relationship binds Paul particularly closely to the church at Philippi (Phil 1:5; 2:1-5; 4:10-20). It was threatened by Paul's imprisonment, since the death of a partner to such an association dissolved the association. Indeed, Paul's imprisonment appears to have been the occasion for an outbreak of factionalism or rivalry between other missionaries in the association (Phil 1:15-17).

If *koinonia* was also a technical term in the missionary efforts of the Johannine churches, then its appearance in 1 Jn provides a clue to the division which has occured. The demand that the author's adherents not involve themselves with the opponents in any way (2 Jn 10-11) implies that rendering them material assistance or hospitality would be entering into *koinonia* with them. The presbyter writes that anyone who greets people comes to share their evil deeds. In a legal association, all the partners to the association share the fruits, or profits, generated by the partnership. Thus, 1 and 2 Jn present a picture of two rival claims to the Johannine *koinonia*. Quite appart from any theological differences between the contending missionaries and teachers, we can see that both are claiming to derive from the "original" Johannnine fellowship. Those to whom 1 and 2 Jn are addressed may well have found themselves uncertain as to which of the contending parties they owed the support they had given to the original group.

Legal parallels as well as the contention generated in the Philippian *koinonia* by Paul's imprisonment, provide a suggestion as to the cause of this division, the death of the leading figure in the Johannine association. Legally, an association dissolved with the death of a partner. If it were to continue, the surviving partners would have to form a new association. Therefore, a likely occasion for the division reflected in the Johannine epistles would be the death of a central figure in the community, who had previously held the association of Johannine Christians together much as Paul did his churches. Since the epistles appear to be composed by a disciple or associate of the evangelist and since the evangelist appears to have been someone distinct from the Beloved Disciple, who was the source of the Johannine tradition (Brown, *Epistles*, 30), it would seem likely that the death of the evangelist caused such a crisis. Jn 21:20-23 shows that the death of the Beloved Disciple led to a reinterpretation of Jesus' sayings. The evangelist may have provided the powerful symbolic expression needed to maintain the Johannine community. This focus made it possible for Johannine churches to continue the tradition of "spirit-filled community" (1 Jn 2:27; 4:4-6) without developing some pattern of teaching offices and authorities that had already taken place in churches of the Pauline and Petrine mission. Perhaps, the evangelist was even regarded as the source of the continued activity of the Spirit/Paraclete in the Johannine church.

1 Jn 2:19 and 2 Jn 7 accuse the opponents of having "gone out" from the fellowship. It would appear that they have established an association for the purpose of preaching and teaching that is independent of that around the presbyter. The death of the evangelist would provide them with the opportunity to do so. The author of 1 Jn consistently reminds his readers that he represents the traditions which they have heard "from the beginning," that is, he claims that his group continues the original association and its teaching. He understands the division within the Johannine community in apocalyptic terms. It is the sign of Satan's activity in attempting to destroy the community of the righteous. He calls those who have formed their own association "antichrists" (1 Jn 2:18,22). He accuses them of denying the fundamental confessions about Jesus, which had bound the community together in its earlier crises (1 Jn 4:1-3). We cannot presume that 1 Jn provides an account of the views held by the opposing teachers and their associates. How-

ever, it seems clear that the division between the two groups was not merely over authority and leadership, though it may have begun in that fashion. Rather, the two associations have also developed the implications of the evangelist's teaching in quite different directions. Often, as we shall see, 1 Jn appears to revert to the images and traditions that are more primitive and closer to an earlier stage of Johannine thought, than the gospel itself. This tendency has even misled some interpreters into insisting that 1 Jn must antedate the gospel. For example, the gospel acknowledges the existence of a future judgment, but insists upon the realization of the promises of eternal life and its converse judgment in the encounter with Jesus. The believer has eternal life (Jn 5:24; 11:26). 1 Jn reverses the emphasis. He insists that judgment remains for Christians and that that judgment depends upon how they conduct their lives (2:6,10,28; 3:2-3,10). The gospel contains the tradition of Jesus' death as atonement (Jn 1:29; 11:51-52) but emphasizes the picture of the crucifixion as Jesus' glorious return to the father (Jn 3:14; 8:28; 12:32-34). 1 Jn, on the other hand, emphasizes the fact that Jesus' death is an atonement for the sin of the world (1 Jn 1:7; 2:2; 3:16; 4:10). These emphases suggest that there is a fundamental disagreement between the two groups over sin and judgment. This disagreement causes the author of 1 Jn to reach back to traditions that are older than the gospel in order to refute the teaching of his opponents (Brown, *Epistles*, 97-100).

Such developments would suggest that the epistles were written sometime after the gospel. Brown suggests 100 C.E. as a plausible date (*Epistles*: 101). The epistles presuppose a network of communities linked by traveling missionaries such as might be found in a city with outlying towns. (Even within the city, one would have a number of household communities.) We can only guess at locale. Brown suggests Ephesus in Asia Minor because other developments in Christianity in this area would fit the Johannine mold. The letters of Ignatius of Antioch (110 C.E.) speak of people who actually do deny the incarnation of Jesus, as 1 Jn accuses his opponents of doing. The picture of the churches of the area in Rev 2-3 shows a Christianity divided by false teaching and what the author considers a moral laxity, though this laxity appears to reflect accomodation to pagan environment that is quite different from what we find in the Johannine epistles (see Perkins, *Revelation*; Collins, *Revelation*). This area spawns certain gnosticizing trends, which could be defended by appeal to the Fourth Gospel, and the emphasis on the Spirit and prophecy in Montanism. The great defender of the Fourth Gospel for the western church, who insisted that it was to be interpreted along the lines set by 1 Jn, Irenaeus of Lyons, also comes from Asia Minor (see Brown, *Epistles*, 100-103).

We do not know what became of the Johannine communities. The use of radical interpretations of the Fourth Gospel in the various gnostic groups suggests one line of development. Those loyal to the interpretation set out by the presbyter of the Johannine epistles do not appear to have formed a distinct type of Christianity. Of course, Ephesus, itself, contained churches in the Pauline tradition. 1 Peter is addressed to communities in rural Asia Minor that reflect a Petrine christianity, as parallels between 1 Peter and Roman sugest. This type of Christianity also was strongly influenced by its heritage of Jewish Christian tradition (see R. Brown and J. Meier, *Antioch & Rome*, 128-39). Brown has suggested that the emphasis on Peter's shepherding role in Jn 21:15-17 may have provided a way into the church order of shepherd/bishop that was becoming common in other churches in Asia Minor. The communities which remained faithful to the tradition as interpreted by the presbyter may have become part of that church structure. Although we do not find direct citation of the gospel in Ignatius of Antioch or Justin Martyr, the Johannine traditions of Jesus as Word of God may have contributed to the theology of the incarnation as it is developed in these writers (Ignatius, *Ephesians* 7:2; 19:1; *Magnesians* 8:2; Brown, *Epistles*, 106-15). Thus, the troubled story of the Johannine churches reflected in the epistles left a rich heritage in second century Christianity.

ONE JOHN

THE FOUNDATION
OF TRUE CHRISTIAN
FELLOWSHIP

Outline

1 JN IS A TREATISE for the instruction of christians in the community; not a personal letter. Since the author relies on repetition, variations on a theme, and word associations, it is difficult to divide the writing into clearly bounded sections. Certain images and metaphors are unevenly distributed throughout the work and may provide some clues. The image of light and darkness as ways of life only occurs up to 2:11. Following 2:29, that image seems to have been replaced by the metaphor of the christian as the one "born from God." Similarly, 2:23-5:12 keep returning to the theme of possessing God and Christ. "Believing" appears in 3:23 to be picked up again in 5:1-13. Chapter 4 has alternative formulations of these themes which focus on doctrine and "confessing Jesus," both of which first emerge as issues after 2:23. The author tends to repeat and to overlap themes so that deciding on precise verse divisions is more difficult than recognizing the major sections. It seems clear that there are divisions around 2:11; 2:28 or 29; 3:23 or 24; and 5:12 or 13, with 5:14-21 as an additional appendix. (Some scholars even attribute it to a different hand.)

Since it is so difficult to arrive at a precise outline on the basis of content or literary features, a common approach has been to outline 1 Jn in terms of alternating ethical and christological sections. The following outline from Schnackenburg's commentary is typical (p. 10):

> Prologue 1:1-4
> A. Ethical 1:5-2:17, walking in light as the sign of true community with God.
>   Christological 2:18-27, belief in Jesus as the foundation of true community with God.
> B. Ethical 2:28-3:24, doing righteousness as the sign that one is "born from God."
>   Christological 4:1-6, the Spirit from God acknowledges Jesus Christ in the flesh.
> C. Both are tied together
>   4:7-21, love as the foundation of faith.
>   5:1-12, faith as the foundation of love.
>   Conclusion 5:13-21.

Brown rejects earlier thematic analysis for a structural parallelism between the epistle and the gospel: Prologue (1:1-4); Part I, God is light & we must walk in light (1:5-3:10); Part II, Gospel, love one another as God loved us in Jesus Christ (3:11-5:12); Conclusion (5:13-21) [*Epistles*: 116-29]. The division at 3:11 has the attractive feature of its repetition of the phrase from 1:5, "this is the preaching (gospel)." However, the author seems to us to be recalling that expression in a context which is directly continuing the image of a "child of the devil" that goes before it in v. 10 and therefore do not find the division as clearly marked as Brown suggests.

Looking at Schnackenburg's outline, we see that the amount of space given to ethical matters is considerably greater than that attached to christology. Therefore, it would seem that the treatise is aimed at instructing those in the community loyal to the presbyter about "how they are to walk." You will notice that Brown's double division finds a central place for paraenesis as well. In his first section, "walking in the light is the key"; in the second, the love command. Reading 1 Jn as a "rule for community life," we suggest the following outline. The commentary on the individual sections will explain our choice of divisions and the problems still inherent in it:

Prologue 1:1-4, remain in fellowship with us.
A. Ethical: Two Ways Paraenesis 1:5-2:17
B. Conflict: Do not be Deceived by the Antichrists 2:18-29.
   vv.28-29 on confidence in the judgment are transitional; they conclude this section and introduce the next.
C. Ethical: Reformulation of "A" 3:1-24
   vv.19-24 are a concluding summary which emphasizes christian confidence before God.
D. Community Rules 4:1-5:12
   4:1-6, antichrists require testing of the spirits (cp. 2:18-27)
   4:7-16a, love in the christian community (cp. 3:1-18)
   4:16b-21, "God is love" (cp. 1:5) as the basis for confidence in the judgment (cp. 2:28-29)
   5:1-12, "Jesus is the Christ" as the basis for being a child of God; for confidence in the judgment and in eternal life (cp. 3:19-24)
   Conclusion 5:13 (cp. Jn 20:30)
   Appendix 5:14-21, rules for prayer and community discipline. (The theme of confidence in judgment occurs here in association with prayer.)

Community Rule and the Crisis of Confidence

1 Jn has a recurring motif of confidence in relation to the judgment and other eschatological rewards such as eternal life. Apocalyptic communities viewed division as a sign of the end-time (1 Jn 4:1-6). Such groups insist that the unity

and religious purity of their community insures that they will survive the coming judgment. Lack of this certainty about their salvation seems to be troubling members of 1 Jn's community. What would cause such a crisis? While the crisis would seem to be related to the opponents' preaching, 1 Jn never castigates them for any explicit moral lapses beyond the failure in mutual love that is reflected in the division of the community. Thus, Brown concludes that the opponents cannot have been moral libertines as some earlier scholars had thought. Instead, he suggests that they taught that moral behavior was indifferent to salvation (*Epistles*: 54-55). Preoccupation with ethics distinguished Christians from the pagan religious cults, where were morally indifferent. It brought Christianity into contact with the popular philosophical traditions (Malherbe, *Social Aspects*: 48f). The importance of the ethical component for the self-definition of early Christianity is so pervasive that we find Brown's suggestion that the opponents were "moral indifferentists" implausible. Therefore, we would agree with those scholars who seek to define the problem as one of moral perfectionism (see J. Bogart, *Orthodox and Heretical Perfectionism*).

Both the gnostic and essene materials provide us with examples of such perfectionism. The essenes insisted that none of the ritual purifications prescribed in the Law would benefit a person who was not purified by strict observance of all the precepts of the Law as interpreted in their tradition. Other, non-observant Jews would find themselves condemned along with the gentiles in the coming judgment. The gnostics, far from being the moral libertines they were often accused of being, often show concern for a strict ascetic practice which would free the soul from the passions and desires that it derives from association with the body. The soul cannot ascend to its heavenly home unless its ties with the evil, material world are broken. They often claim that christian baptism is useless; true perfection must be attained by freeing one's soul from passion and attachment to the things of this world.

The anxiety that seems to have been engendered by the "perfectionist" preaching of the opponents may have been intensified by the Johannine tradition itself. The gospel presents the sum total of Jesus' ethical teaching in the command to "love one another"—a tradition continued in the paraenesis of 1 Jn. If the opponents held up as the only true standard of perfection either a christian *halachah* on the analogy with judaism or an ascetic perfection of a "passionless" soul on the analogy with gnosticism and the pagan philosophical praxis from which gnostics derived their view, then the Johannine christians could well have become anxious about their status in the judgment because they lacked any standard for measurement to hold up against these other claims. 1 Jn seeks to deal with their concern by explaining that the love of God shown in Jesus is the true foundation of their community and source of Christian sinlessness. He continues to hold up the love commandment as the one norm of behavior and relationship to God.

REMAIN IN FELLOWSHIP WITH US.
1:1-4.

> **1** That which was from the beginning, which we have heard, which we have seen with our eyes, which we have looked upon and touched with our hands, concerning the word of life—²the life was made manifest, and we saw it, and testify to it, and proclaim to you the eternal life which was with the Father and was made manifest to us—³that which we have seen and heard we proclaim also to you, so that you may have fellowship with us; and our fellowship is with the Father and with his Son Jesus Christ. ⁴And we are writing this that our joy may be complete.

The language of the fourth gospel pervades this section, since it clearly stands at the foundation of the community's discourse. Obvious parallels to the prologue of the gospel are found in the images of beginning, word and life in the presence of God (see the detailed chart in Brown, *Epistles*: 176). There these metaphors characterized the word of God about to be made manifest in a hostile world. Here, the author of 1 Jn looks back on that manifestation as the foundation of the christian community, which he is hoping to hold together by his exhortation.

Metaphors from elsewhere in the gospel also occur in this section. Unless we pick them up, we miss the full impact of what the author is saying. The expression "from the beginning" appears in two different contexts in the gospel. It can refer to the testimony to be given by the disciples, who are Jesus' witnesses "from the beginning" (Jn 15:27). In Jn 15:11 Jesus tells his disciples that he has spoken with them so that "their joy may be full" (cf. 16:20-24; 17:13). You can see from 1 Jn 1:4 that the author has framed the introduction by allusion to these two passages. His audience is to be sure that his and their joy will be full just as Jesus has promised.

"From the beginning" also appears in a negative context. In Jn 8:44 it designates the true nature of the opposition to Jesus: the devil is a liar "from the beginning." 1 Jn 3:8 picks up that passage from the gospel. The devil is a sinner "from the beginning," and Jesus has appeared (= "made manifest" of v.2) to destroy his works. The expression "made manifest" in v.2 often occurs in the gospel in association with the works of Jesus showing the Father to those who have faith to see Jesus' true identity (Jn 2:11; 9:3; 7:4, in reference to an inappropriate demand for such a showing; 17:6, Jesus has "made manifest" the Father's name to the disciples). Or, it may refer to human actions whose true nature is "made manifest" by the appearance of Jesus as light (3:21). Similar usage is found in 1 Jn. "Made manifest" can refer to Jesus' coming as savior (1 Jn 3:5,8). Or, it can refer to the distinction between people that is now at issue: the true children of God who remain in fellowship with the author and the tradition "from the beginning" as opposed to those who have departed from their community (2:19, 28; 3:10).

Emphasis on the "appearing" of Jesus represents an important theological development made by the Johannine tradition. Pauline theology stresses the death and resurrection of Jesus as the saving event. The Johannine tradition has not lost that traditional interpretation of the death of Jesus (cf. Jn 12:46; 1 Jn 4:9,14; 5:6); but it has broadened the concept of saving event to include the whole life of Jesus—the power of eternal, divine life has come into the cosmos (1 Jn 2:17 ; see Schnackenburg: 62f). The saving significance of Jesus' coming from the Father is not reduced to any part of his activity. It is not simply bringing revelation about God—a reduction popular among gnostics for whom the death of Jesus has no relation to our salvation.

The tradition of testimony about what has happened in Jesus becomes especially important in christian communities in which most or all members have not known either Jesus or any of the original disciples. The fourth gospel concludes with a benediction for those who have believed without seeing (20:29). Jn 17:20-23 gives these later christians the same mission of testimony and the same glory, unity and love with Father and Son that was bestowed on the original disciples (see Perkins: 197-205). The fourth gospel makes it clear that later christians stand in the same relation to Jesus and the Father as the first disciples because of the presence of Jesus in the testimony of the community and the eucharist, a presence which is not caught in the limits of historical time (Perkins: 241f). 1 Jn does not want christians to lose sight of the fact that everything they now experience as coming from Jesus depends on their continuing in continuity with him as he was made manifest to those first witnesses. Remember, when the author of 1 Jn speaks about what is seen and touched, he is not referring to the kind of facts about Jesus we would have if people had been able to videotape his life and hand the tapes on to us. The gospel makes it clear that many people who saw and heard Jesus, even those who witnessed his miracles, did not become believers (e.g. 2:22f). They did not see that he was from God. Only those who could see Jesus' works as manifesting the glory of God would become witnesses to him (2:11).

Brown suggests that the epistles now use "we" to refer to that group of disciples who, like the author of the letter, stand in a special relationship to the Beloved Disciple. This school of tradition-bearers carries the 'eye-witness' testimony into the audience's present (*Epistles*: 158-61).

Commentators sometimes assume that the language about "seeing, hearing and touching" Jesus was directed against gnostics who denied the reality of Jesus. That approach flounders on the fact that gnostics never deny that Jesus has a body which can be seen, handled and touched. A 2nd century gnostic work, the *Gospel of Truth* (GTr) even alludes to this passage from 1 Jn in support of the gnostic preaching about Jesus (CG I *3* 30,27-31,20; *NHLE*: 43f). (See Bibliography: Robinson.) Joy characterizes the gnostic reception of salvation. They are encouraged to bear witness to the truth about Jesus. And, finally, the Father's love for them makes gnostics true brothers and children of the Father (43,5-24; *NHLE* 49). But the gnostics also claim that Jesus brought a new revelation about the Father, which was not known before and which is only attainable to those who are gnostics. Sometimes, they insist that Jesus did not reveal the true nature of the Father or his own glory to the disciples until after the resurrection. Everything reported about the earthly life and teaching of Jesus would have to be interpreted in the light of that esoteric revelation. 1 Jn provides the basis for Christians to deny any such attempts to sever their image of Jesus as savior from the earthly Jesus. The epistle uses the language of "seeing, hearing and touching" to evoke personal presence and to establish the claim that only their tradition derives from that presence. In the Johannine tradition, there is no break between the earthly and risen Jesus or between Jesus and what the community came to understand about him through the spirit (e.g. Jn 14:26; 16:13).

The Johannine tradition is famous for its expressions of the unity of believers with each other and with the Father and Son.

The word *koinonia*, fellowship, only occurs here (v.4) and in the introduction to the next section (vv.6f). Otherwise, the author uses more characteristically Johannine expressions. We have seen that the Johannine community faced a severe threat to its unity. Since the Johannine tradition had found in the earlier situation of persecution that unity between believers and God, the Son and the Spirit to be its foundation, this new division threatened the roots of the community. For the Johannine tradition, Jesus, himself, is the only source of light, truth, glory, and life. The most characteristic Johannine expression is "remain or abide in." Throughout the gospel remaining in or with Jesus is used to mean staying with him as disciple rather than being led to reject him by the jewish opposition (e.g. 15:4; Perkins: 173). That way of speaking can easily be carried over into this new situation in which some christians seem to form a separate group and to encourage other members of Johannine communities to follow their lead. Two aspects of discipleship are associated with expressions of "remaining or abiding": sticking with the teaching about Jesus (1 Jn 2:24,27f; 2 Jn 9), and leading a life appropriate to a believer, one of mutual love (2:6; 3:6; 4:12). 1 Jn uses the related expression "to be in God" in a similar way (2:5; 5:20). Sometimes he varies the metaphor by speaking of abiding in an attribute of the Father: truth (1:8; 2:4); his word (1:10; 2:14); his seed (3:9); eternal life (3:15); love (4:12). The carefully constructed allusions to the fourth gospel in this section stress the fact that the fellowship shared by the author and his audience is grounded in Jesus, himself. Thus, the author penetrates to the theological foundations of the community's unity. He does not permit the reader to think that it does not matter whether one belongs to the fellowship of the author or that of the opponents, a conclusion one might draw from the merely sociological use of *koinonia* language in the missionary context. (Brown suggests that the author's emphasis, here, betrays an attraction for the secessionist position on the part of the audience [*Epistles*: 185-87]. We are more hesitant to use the audience evoked by the author to describe the actual situation of the community.)

WALKING IN THE LIGHT.
1:5-2:17.

The first major section of 1 Jn presents fellowship as remaining in the community in which there is true forgiveness of sin. Remaining in that community implies love for its members. The language of this section: dualistic contrast between light and darkness as ways of life; concern with the ethical purity of the community, and allusion to the final judgment of God, fits a pattern of jewish and early christian ethical preaching known as "two ways." Perhaps the best known jewish example is found in the community rule from Qumran. You will notice that the community rule plays an important part in identifying the member of the group. Members are exhorted to love their brethren, the "sons of light," and to hate outsiders, "the sons of darkness," (1 QS 1.9f). 1 QS 3.13-4.26 contain two ways teaching under the head of the two spirits which struggle for humanity's allegiance. Notice that the final destruction of sinfulness, the spirit of perversity, is associated with the cleansing action of the spirit of God, which is compared to the ritual waters of purification (4.19-23). Gal 5:17-24, a short christian example, show the features common to such exhortation: (1) dualistic introduction, spirit/flesh (vv.17f); (2) double catalogue of virtues and vices (vv.19-21a,22f); (3) eschatological reference (21b,24). Other early christian examples are found in the Apostolic Fathers, *Barnabas* 18.1-21.9 and *Didache* 1.1-6.2. If you compare these, you will notice that in *Didache* the concern with light and darkness and angelic powers characteristic of 1 QS and *Barnabas* has been replaced by the metaphors of life and death. You will also notice that the later christian authors have used teaching of Jesus from the synoptic tradition as an important component of the content of their paraenesis. Baptism and confession of sin still appear in the context of "two ways" exhortation, thus suggesting that its original context was the initiation of new members into the community. The Qumran example is clearly associated with the initiation ritual, which also required confession of sinfulness by the members (1 QS 1.24f; also CD 20:28b). Here in 1 Jn 1:8-10, we find confession of sinfulness as part of the exhortation to "walk in light." The dualistic division between members of the community and outsiders who "walk in darkness," suggests that this Johannine exhortation also derives from an initiatory context. It defined the initiate as set apart, as a member of those saved by the coming of Jesus.

Though one cannot accept Bultmann's reconstruction of a source document behind this part of 1 Jn (Bultmann: 18), the insight that the author is using material from another context does seem correct. 1 Jn is referring back to preaching which his audience knows from another context, probably their initiation into the Johannine community. The author wishes to appeal to the language of christian initiation in such a way as to make casual dividing of that fellowship impossible. A person who does not remain within it cannot have forgiveness of sin and righteousness from God.

This emphasis is enhanced by the peculiarity of Johannine "two ways" exhortation. Although there are general references to commandments in the plural (e.g. 1 Jn 2:3f; cp. Jn 15:10), only one commandment is ever stated, love the brethren (2:7). The Johannine gospel has a similar movement. Commandments in the plural are mentioned; but only the love command is explicitly given as such (Jn 15:10-12; also 13:34 and 14:15,21). It is clear that the Johannine tradition understands love as the defining characteristic of its community. In the gospel, this "love one another" is emphasized in the face of external hostility and persecution, which threatens to break up the community and has caused some members to leave. These memories from the past were well-engrained in the language and memories of later christians, who had not lived through them, by the repetition of the gospel stories. 1 Jn can now invoke them to address the new situation in which people are leaving as a result of internal division rather than external persecution.

1:5 *God is Light*

> ⁵This is the message we have heard from him and proclaim to you, that God is light and in him is no darkness at all.

The section begins with an appeal to an accepted metaphor for God, light. The image of the divine as light was widespread in both hellenistic pagan and jewish piety. The word translated "message," *angelia*, may be the Johannine equivalent of the more familiar Pauline "gospel," *euangelion* (Brown, *Epistles*, 192-93). It reappears in 3:11 where the *angelia* heard from the beginning is the love command. After the prologue to the work, we might have expected "message" to have been followed by "from the beginning" rather than the somewhat vague "from him." "From him" is probably intended to be equivalent to the expression "from the beginning" and to indicate that what the author is about to present is in continuity with what has come from Jesus through the testimony in the community. It could not indicate an allusion to the teaching of Jesus, since the metaphor appears neither in the synoptic tradition nor in the fourth gospel. Perhaps, the readers of 1 Jn would even have identified *angelia* with the Fourth Gospel, itself (Brown, *Epistles*: 193). The latter, in fact, stresses Jesus as light of the world. It uses light as symbol of his saving presence (Jn 1:4,5,9; 8:12; 9:5; 14:9).

1 Jn typically focuses on God the Father where the gospel might have emphasized Jesus as revelation of the Father. 1 Jn uses titles for Jesus which belong to christian tradition earlier than the gospel and which might have been applied to any righteous person (cf. 1 Jn 2:7f) without

evoking the charges of blasphemous identification of a human being with God raised in the gospel. Jesus is messiah (2:22), son (1:3; 3:23), sin-offering (1:7; 2:2; 4:10), and advocate (2:1). This treatment of Jesus has led some interpreters to suggest that 1 Jn was written before the gospel and the development of its christology. However, allusions to the gospel in 1 Jn and the reflection of the gospel's christology in the language of dwelling with Father and Son lead us to reject that view. Instead, 1 Jn shows us that it was possible to have a picture of Jesus' divinity such as is presented in the fourth gospel without eclipsing the Father's place in christian life and reflection. All too many christians today identify Jesus with God in such a way that they do worship only one God, Jesus. 1 Jn does not fall into the kind of di-theism claimed by the jewish opponents of christianity in the gospel controversies. If anything, the powerfully sketched picture of Jesus in the gospel had revitalized confidence that God was active for the salvation of those who trusted in him. When applied to Jesus in the gospel, light imagery symbolized his revelation as saving humanity. Applied to the Father, here, it symbolizes the perfection and purity of his divinity. But unlike many forms of hellenistic and gnostic piety, association of light with divine being did not mean that people were to seek a personal, private, interior vision of that divine light. It meant, as the author will go on to spell out, that they were to conduct their lives in obedience and fidelity to the community which that God had acted to establish (1:6f; 2:10f).

1:6-10 *Fellowship of Those who Walk in the Light*

⁶If we say we have fellowship with him while we walk in darkness, we lie and do not live according to the truth; ⁷but if we walk in the light, as he is in the light, we have fellowship with one another, and the blood of Jesus his Son cleanses us from all sin. ⁸If we say we have no sin, we deceive ourselves, and the truth is not in us. ⁹If we confess our sins, he is faithful and just, and will forgive

our sins and cleanse us from all unrighteousness. [10]If we say we have not sinned, we make him a liar, and his word is not in us.

This string of conditional sentences is a fine example of the author's use of antithetical parallelism. Statements of erroneous views, "if we say that . . . ," and their consequences alternate with presentation of the true action of christians, walking in the light, confession of sinfulness, and the resulting fellowship and forgiveness. Just as the whole section was introduced by a statement characterizing divine being, "God is light," so each statement about true christian action is associated with another attribute of God himself. He is "in the light" (v.7; = "is light" v.5), and he is "faithful" and "just" (v.9; cf. Exod 34:6f; Dt 32:4). Verse 10 concludes the section and forms an *inclusio* with v.6.

We saw that the initiatory setting of two ways paraenesis in both judaism and early christianity included confession of sin. The essene neophyte is about to be cleansed (1 QS 1.16; 3:12; CD 20:28f) by entry into the community of the elect. Christian tradition has always associated baptism with forgiveness of sins (Mk 1:5; Mt 3:6). 1 Pet 2:9b speaks of the new convert from paganism as one called out of darkness into the light of God. And Eph 5:8-13 encourages christians not to associate with any kind of immorality by referring back to their baptism as coming from darkness into the light given by Christ. They are exhorted to "walk as children of light" (8b; cp. 1 Jn 1:7a). These parallels clearly indicate that 1 Jn is recalling the baptismal paraenesis of his community.

Early christians went beyond associating forgiveness with baptism to claim that forgiveness of sin was effected by the death of Jesus. Originally, the idea that the death of Jesus was a sacrifice for sin may have originated in the gentile mission. The gentiles who had been living lives totally separated from God (the darkness of Eph and 1 Pet) and without access to the means of salvation and atonement he had given the jewish people in the Law, now had a sacrifice to atone for their sins. Paul (Rom 3:21-25) expands such a tradition to present Jesus as the sin-offering for all christians both jews and gentiles. The gentiles need his gift of righteousness because of their long history of turning away from God; the jews because they have constantly been disobedient and broken the covenant God had made with them. So now God has provided all of humanity with a new righteousness, one which does not make any distinction between jew and gentile (see also Rom 5:8-11; Eph 1:7; Col 1:20-22; and similar expressions in non-Pauline writings, Heb 1:3; 9:12; 1 Pet 1:19). 1 Cor 15:3 shows that by the 50s A.D. the death of Christ "for sins" was a standard part of christian belief (as does its formulaic use in epistolary introductions like Gal 1:4 and 1 Pet 1:2). The fourth gospel did not exploit the image of the death of Jesus as sacrifice however. There Jesus lays down his life as part of a plan by which that death is his exaltation and return to the glory he had with the Father. However, the sacrificial interpretation is mentioned. Reference to Jesus as "lamb of God" 1:29 recalls other early christian sacrificial interpretations (e.g. Heb 9:12; 1 Pet 1:19; Rev 7:9). Jn 11:50 refers to the death of Jesus "for the people" as making possible the incorporation of the gentiles into the people of God. Therefore, such language about the death of Jesus was probably always part of the paraenesis of the community.

The "word of God" negated by refusal to acknowledge the need for cleansing from sin effected by Christ (v. 10) does not refer to the pre-existent word, but to God's word of promise. The positive teaching about forgiveness in this passage is clear enough. One would also expect the exhortation to a new life of holiness such as that in v.6 (cp. the paraenesis in Eph 5:8-13). When people misinterpreted the "freedom from sin" granted in baptism to mean that Christians were free to do anything they chose, New Testament authors always reminded them that their conduct had to correspond to the new reality given in baptism. But they do not go to the extent that the essene community does in trying to embody perfect holiness and purity in the community through a high standard of obedience to the Law; careful ranking of members; punishments for infractions (cf. 1 QS 1.24-26; 6.24-7.25). Even the essene admits that real purification from sin is not within the realm of mere human achievement but must depend upon the eschatological gift of the spirit of God.

The puzzle in this section lies in the false claims of sinlessness reported in vv. 8 and 10. Nothing in the context suggests that members of the Johannine community were following a libertine interpretation of christianity such as may have been the case among some of Paul's gentile converts. Therefore, we should probably not interpret these verses to mean that the author's opponents were asserting that it was impossible for a christian to commit sin. Such charges were sometimes made against gnostics. The evidence of our gnostic writings, however, suggests that the problem might have been a claim to perfection based on moral and ascetic seriousness; a seriousness which led to denial of a divine forgiveness mediated by baptism or the sacrificial death of Jesus. Such writings insist that each person must achieve perfection through his or her knowledge and ascetic practice. One must conquer the passions of the soul and become free from attachment to the material world or the body. Several late 2nd century or 3rd century gnostic texts explicitly attack the orthodox claim that the death of Jesus atones for sin. A tract which preaches severe asceticism as the way to salvation, *Testimony of Truth*, says that any God who would demand a human sacrifice would be vain-glorious, and could not be the true God (CG IX *3* 33,19-21; *NHLE*: 408). Another, less concerned with asceticism than with gnostic survival in the face of christian persecution, attacks the orthodox for thinking that they can be saved and become pure by "cleaving to the name of a dead man" (*Apocalypse of Peter* CG VII *3* 70,10-15; *NHLE*: 341). These examples make it clear that it was possible to reject the association of forgiveness of sins with the death of Jesus out of a concern for moral perfection and asceticism. Such a claim did not imply moral laxity or the claim that gnostics cannot sin no matter what they do. Since the fourth gospel had not emphasized sacrificial imagery in depicting the death of Jesus, it would have been easy for members of the Johannine community to claim that their quest for perfection was in line with the traditional picture of a Jesus who is free from the passions and snares of the world. The author of 1 Jn seems to have caricatured their position by implying that it was a claim to present and past sinlessness.

Brown proposes to solve the difficulties of v. 8a by translating the expression "have sin" (*hamartian echein*) as "be guilty of sin." He points to the use of the expression in the gospel (Jn 9:41; 15:22,24; 19:11) for the existing sin of those who are blind to Jesus' message and respond by persecuting either Jesus or his followers (*Epistles*: 205-206). This expression parallels the opponents with those who rejected Jesus in the gospel. Verses 9 and 10 seem to have transformed an baptismal confession of sin (cf. Mk 1:5; Matt 3:6; Acts 19:18; *Didache* 4:14) into a description of the post-baptismal life of the Christian. It woud appear that there was some form of public acknowledgement of sin within the community (also see Jas 5:16; *Didache* 14:1; Brown, *Epistles*, 208-12). Perhaps, the opponents have also rejected this practice. If they appealed to the Fourth Gospel, they might have pointed to its assertion that the person who believes in Jesus has no sin; has already passed through judgment (3:18; 5:24; Brown, [*Epistles*: 230-42], reconstructs the opponents' position to be one which asserted that one's ethical behavior was irrelevant to salvation.).

2:1-2 Jesus our Advocate

> **2** My little children, I am writing this to you so that you may not sin; but if any one does sin, we have an advocate with the Father, Jesus Christ the righteous; [2]and he is the expiation for our sins, and not for ours only but also for the sins of the whole world.

1 Jn now turns from the application of baptismal paraenesis against his opponents to address his audience. The expression "little children," first used here, will become common (2:12,28; 3:7,18; 4:4; 5:21). In wisdom literature, the address "my son" or "my child" indicates the teacher/ pupil relationship between the sage and those he is instructing. The phrase "little children" occurs once in the fourth gospel at the beginning of the farewell discourses. Jesus uses it when he turns to address his true disciples after the betrayer has gone out (13:33). In the next verse he introduces the commandment of love for one another (13:34). Thus, 1 Jn is able to evoke the solemn context of Jesus' final legacy to his faithful disciples by using this instruction. He will shortly remind them specifically of the love command.

Jesus as Advocate

The expression "advocate" or *paraclete* only occurs here and in the fourth gospel. The sayings about the paraclete in chapters 14-16 of the gospel show a complex history of development. Johannine use of the term may have first come into play during controversy with the jews. Jn 5:45 attacks that confidence by claiming that Moses is on the side of Jesus. He will not intercede for the jews who reject Jesus but will turn and accuse them. Jesus is consistently portrayed as greater than Moses (Jn 1:17f) so it is not surprising that he should take on the function of heavenly advocate as well.

Just as was the case with christological titles, the picture of the paraclete in the gospel is more complex than 1 Jn's appeal to Jesus as heavenly advocate. There, the paraclete stands almost as an independent figure whose activity is associated with the life of the community in the world rather than with the heavenly presence of Jesus at God's right hand. In Jn 16, the paraclete fulfils the functions that a more traditional eschatology expected of the Son of Man's glorious return in judgment. Those who have rejected Jesus stand condemned (16:7-10), and christians learn that all the messianic prophecies have been fulfilled in Jesus (16:13). In Jn 15:26, like the spirit in the synoptic tradition, the paraclete assists christians who must testify to their faith in Jesus. In chapter 14, the image of the paraclete seems to be convertible with the in-dwelling language that expresses the presence of Father and Son to the community (see Perkins: 189-96). The polemic formulations of chapters 15 & 16 are clearly not relevant to the situation in 1 Jn, and the author prefers the indwelling expressions for divine presence. Many commentators assume that the author is basing his teaching on the experience of the paraclete in the community without realizing that "paraclete" was not a fixed figure in Johannine language but a fluid symbol which could take on different functions in different contexts. 1 Jn suggests that the community commonly spoke of Jesus as the heavenly paraclete.

Jesus can be conceived as a heavenly advocate like Moses without associating that function with his death for sins. 1 Jn insists that it is precisely his death for the sin of the world which underlies his present intercession for the community. A similar image of Jesus occurs in the letter to the Hebrews. The exalted Jesus, who made the perfect sacrifice for sins in his death, now intercedes in heaven (Heb 7:25-27). Thus, the Johannine picture of Jesus as advocate has appropriated the larger picture of Jesus' atoning death. "World" in v.2 is not a symbol of all that is hostile to God as it is in 2:15-17 but simply refers to all of humanity (as in Jn 1:29; 3:16f; 4:42; 12:47). Later gnostic evidence shows that they could accept the picture of Jesus as heavenly advocate for sin (*Apocryphon of James* CG I 2 11,4-6; *NHLE*: 34) without an associated doctrine of the death of Jesus as atonement. This particular gnostic writing makes extensive use of Johannine traditions apparently in response to orthodox polemic against the gnostics. If you read it, you will notice that the discussion of sin which follows on the assertion that Jesus will be heavenly intercessor depends upon an anthropology of spirit—soul—body. A soul filled with the spirit will be able to keep the body from sin; the body itself is not an object of salvation. Jesus' prayers may attain forgiveness for the gnostic, but the real victory over sin is not achieved by such intercession. It must be won in the individual spirit—soul. 1 Jn, on the other hand, has no such anthropological analysis. Jesus' intercession and atoning death make forgiveness a permanent reality within the community. That forgiveness is experienced any time the christian falls short of the perfection which he or she seeks. Brown suggests that the expression "an atonement. . . world" may be an echo of the Johannine eucharistic formula (cf. Jn 6:51). We also find Jesus' death represented as an atonement for sin in Rom 3:24-25. The theme of Jesus' death as atonement plays a minor role in the gospel where John the Baptist proclaims Jesus lamb of God (1:29), but it is developed extensively in Revelation (cf. 5:6). Thus, the author would seem to be reaching back to an early stage of the tradition for this picture of Jesus' death as atonement (Brown, *Epistles*, 240).

2:3-6 Keep his Commandments

> ³And by this we may be sure that we know him, if we keep his commandments. ⁴He who says, "I know him" but disobeys his commandments is a liar, and the truth is not in him; ⁵but whoever keeps his word, in him truly love for God is perfected. By this we may be sure that we are in him: ⁶he who says he abides in him ought to walk in the same way in which he walked.

The author goes on to exhort his audience not to sin. The presence of forgiveness in the community is not a license to let up on one's efforts to "keep his commandments." The expression "I have known him (= God)" in v. 4 has led many interpreters to assume that the author's opponents claimed a direct vision or knowledge of God as the goal of religious perfection; a vision which negated concern for ethical behavior in the community. If the expression "I have known him" is a slogan of the author's opponents, one should interpret it along the line of Schnackenburg's suggestion (p. 99) that the crucial difference in revelation between the two sides is focused by 1 Jn's insistence that *Jesus was sent by the Father to make atonement for sin in the flesh*. Brown suggests that the author is continuing his correction of a false interpretation of the prologue to the gospel of John, which contrasts the world which does not "know him" (1:10) with those who accept the revelation of the light and become children of God (1:12-13). The author insists upon the Old Testament traditions that associate "knowing God" with keeping God's commandments (*Epistles*: 278-81).

However, we favor an alternate hypothesis that the expression "I have known God" was not a slogan of the opponents but one that had developed within the Johannine tradition. Jesus says to Thomas in Jn 14:7: "If you had known me, you would have known my Father also; henceforth you know him and you have seen him." We suggest that the expression "ones who know God" came to be used to characterize the knowledge of God belonging to the members of the Johannine community during its conflict with judaism and does not refer to any particular doctrine of the present opponents. In this section, the author is reformulating the baptismal paraenesis of 1:5-7. The return to the expression "walk" in v.6 refers back to that section.

Further allusions to the farewell discourses broaden the imagery of the treatise and prepare for the introduction of the new commandment in vv.7-11. Verse 5 assures us that the love of God is perfected in the person who keeps his (= Jesus') word (cf. Jn 8:51f; 14:23f). The RSV has translated the genitive expression "love of God" as "love for God" as though it referred to human love directed toward God. However, the expression may just as well refer to the subject of love, that is the object of the love but to its subject, that is, to God as the one who loves humanity (cf. 1 Jn 4:8,16,20; 5:2f). Further support for that interpretation may be derived from the farewell discourses. We suggest that this verse is an alternative formulation of the indwelling language of Jn 14:23f: "If someone loves me, he will keep my word, and my Father

will love him, and we will come and make our home with
him." The individual's love is directed toward Jesus in keeping his word, and toward other christians. For the Johannine tradition, the perfection of God's love for humanity
is attained in the community of those among whom the
Father and Son dwell.

The concluding verse of the section appeals to Jesus'
"walking" as an example for the christian life. The expression "abide in" while equivalent to the "be in" of the previous
verse very often carries overtones of adversity: one remains
a disciple of Jesus despite hostility or external pressure.
The allusion to Jesus' example may be intended to recall
Jesus' own appeal to his example in the footwashing story
(Jn 13:15). That story is particularly apt in this context,
since the gospel uses it as the preparation for Jesus' com-
missioning his true disciples to take over the task of bearing
testimony, of being the "ones sent by Jesus" (13:16,20).

2:7-11 The New Commandment

> [7]Beloved, I am writing you no new commandment,
> but an old commandment which you had from the
> beginning; the old commandment is the word which you
> have heard. [8]Yet I am writing you a new commandment,
> which is true in him and in you, because the darkness is
> passing away and the true light is already shining. [9]He
> who says he is in the light and hates his brother is in the
> darkness still. [10]He who loves his brother abides in the
> light, and in it there is no cause for stumbling. [11]But he
> who hates his brother is in the darkness and walks in the
> darkness, and does not know where he is going, because
> the darkness has blinded his eyes.

All the allusions to the farewell discourses now break
out into a clear reference to Jesus' commandment of love as
the characteristic of his community. At the same time, that
"new" commandment is also part of the testimony to which
the tradition has witnessed "from the beginning." It is the
epitome of Johannine paraenesis. "From the beginning"

carries overtones from 1:1 of being part of the tradition from Jesus, but its more immediate reference is to the beginning of the audience's own instruction as christians. The author is still recalling their baptismal paraenesis. "Beloved" seems to have been a common form of address in early christianity (1 Jn 3:2,21; 4:1,7,11: 2 Jn 2,5,11; cp. Rom 12:19; 2 Cor 7:1). Those who hold that the entire section is aimed directly at the opponents suggest that the author is speaking of the commandment as "old" to distinguish it from the doctrinal innovations of the gnosticizing group (cp. 2 Jn 9). We think that the author is not yet speaking about his opponents but is using baptismal paraenesis to establish a common ground between himself and his audience as required by the rhetorical tradition. (Brown, [*Epistles*: 285-88], takes the section as an interpretation of the gospel's prologue against the opponents.) "Old" emphasizes the importance of Jesus' "new" commandment (Jn 13:34) as the foundation of the community. The next verse turns to the "newness" of that commandment: it represents the fulfilment of the eschatological promise of light. Early christian preaching frequently spoke of the life of christians being lived in light, light which was to be fully realized at Jesus' return. They could live in that light because the darkness of a sinful world was already passing away. We have seen this use of "light" in our discussion of Eph 5:8-14 (see above on 1 Jn 1:6-10). You can also find it in 1 Thess 5:4-10 and Rom 13:11f.

Some gnostic ascetics took over this language of apocalyptic paraenesis. In *Thomas the Contender*, for example, Jesus the revealer is the true light which shines to call people out of the "world of bestiality," away from the flesh and sufferings and passions of the body, into union with him (CG II 7 139,31-140,5; 145,8-15; *NHLE*: 190; 194). 1 Jn, of course, has no such ascetic interpretation of the symbol.

Rather than continuing his earlier reference to God as light, 1 Jn seems to have shifted to the gospel's image of Jesus as the light of the believer in the world (Jn 8:12; 9:5; 12:46). Verses 9-11 refer to Jesus' claim to be the light in which the believer abides, and also to a simile used for his presence in the world at Jn 11:9: the person who walks by day does not stumble; he who walks at night does because he does not have light *in himself*. The RSV has obscured this allusion by opting to translate the *en auto* of v.10b as "in it" rather than "in himself" though they note the other possibilty. Their translation gives a smoother reading to v.10b but hides the allusion. Verse 11 combines this reference with another saying about Jesus as light from Jn 12:35: the one who walks in darkness "does not know where he is going." Such combinations are a common feature of oral preaching and teaching such as the author has been using throughout.

The real exegetical difficulty in these verses is understanding the negative formulation of the love commandment as a prohibition against "hating one's brother." The only references to hatred in the fourth gospel are to that directed at christians from the outside (as also in 1 Jn 3:13). The community rule at Qumran does instruct people to love the members of the sect and hate outsiders (1 QS 1.2f; 9.16, 21f), but such expressions are not paralleled in the New Testament. The usual meaning of "brother" in the New Testament is "fellow christian," which also seems to be the meaning of the injunction to "love one another" in the Johannine formulation of the love command (Jn 13:34; 15:12-17), since only Jesus' friends, the circle of those he has just purified (13:10) receive the teaching. (Also see the "love one another/the brethren" in 1 Jn 3:11,13,15,23; 4:7,11,12,20f; 2 Jn 5). But some commentators think that 1 Jn may have a wider context of christian love—perhaps the injunction to love one's enemies—in mind. They point to 1 Jn 4:21 where the combination of love of God and brother could be a Johannine translation of the double command of love of God and neighbor. Thus, they would like to see this teaching as a reference to love of neighbor which is not limited to the christian community.

The issue is far from clear. 1 Jn 3:17 speaks of the necessity of helping a brother in need in a context which even those who favor a wider interpretation of the love command admit must refers to christians. Jas 2:14-17 shows that such paraenesis was common in early christian preaching. In order to understand what is involved in this teaching, we must remember that the needs of the poor were dealt with through socially established networks of family, trade associations (often provided for one's burial), or attachment to a rich person as patron. Jews embodied the Old Testament teaching of care for the poor among their people by dispensing charity through the synagogue. You can see that it would be necessary for christians to come up with their own forms of social support for members whose conversion left them without the traditional means of assistance. The Johannine community as a whole may have been forced to focus on "love for one another" in a special way during the persecution at the time the gospel was written. One common form of such early christian "love for one another" was hospitality. Missionaries and other christians who had to travel sought the hospitality of churches in the cities to which they went. Travelers in the ancient world would commonly seek out the area of a city where people from their home country had settled—perhaps organized around worship of a native deity, or trade association, or in the case of Jews a local synagogue. 3 Jn deals with a crisis caused by a failure to respond to such a request for hospitality. Thus, it seems to us that 1 Jn is consistently using the love command to refer to fellow christians, and that this command had achieved its prominent place in the community during the period of persecution when members lost their traditional support (as in the story of Jn 9). However, in the social context of these Johannine Christians the requirement to love one's fellow christian in the same way that traditional loyalties demanded one treat a member of one's family had the same broadening effect of the general injunction to love one's enemies—or that demands that christians be concerned for the suffering and oppressed no matter who they are have today. A person had to go beyond some very strong traditional loyalties to family, friends, social class, trade, etc. to meet the demands of this new community. The command to "love one another" is not a case of retreating from the wider "love your enemies" into a world of those with whom one is familiar and comfortable as it might be today.

2:12-14 The Victory You have Won

> [12]I am writing to you, little children, because your sins are forgiven for his sake. [13]I am writing you, fathers, because you know him who is from the beginning. I am writing to you, young men, because you have overcome the evil one. I write to you, children, because you know the Father. [14]I write to you, fathers, because you know him who is from the beginning. I write to you, young men, because you are strong, and the word of God abides in you, and you have overcome the evil one.

The author breaks into chant-like formulae to remind his audience that they are not among those walking in darkness because they have conquered sinfulness through the forgiveness received in Jesus. The expressions "father, young men, children" link this section with a common literary form in early christian preaching, the "household code." In such "codes," the preacher would set out the duties of each class of people in the congregation in turn (e.g. Eph 5:22-6:9; Col 3:18-4:1). The earlier part of the Ephesian material has already provided parallels to the use of "two ways" in 1 Jn. Since that "two ways" paraenesis is followed by a household code, we suspect that the author has chosen his style of speaking because such a code was part of the traditional paraenesis of the Johannine community as well. But he does not, in fact, set out a table of duties. Instead, he once again invokes the language of the fourth gospel to assure his readers that they have won the promised victory through their faith. His aim seems to be to bring the audience to a conviction of the superiority of their faith before he turns to deal directly with the threats to it in 2:18.

Verse 12 addresses all believers. They have received forgiveness both through baptism and through their continued presence in the community as the author has already explained. The RSV rendering of the phrase which says literally "for the sake of his name" as "for his sake" obscures the author's allusion to Jn 1:12: those who believe in his name are children of God (cf. 3:18). None of the attempts by exegetes to attach the remaining terms to specific groups or officials within the community (i.e. fathers=elders) has won much support. Using other analogies to young and elders for divisions within a community (1 QS 6:13-24; 1 Pet 2:2; 1 Cor 3:1; 4:15), Brown concludes that it is possible that the terms referred to two groups within the community. However, it is impossible to specify the function of such titles (*Epistles*: 297-300). It seems that the various designations derive from the literary form the author is using, while the content of the victory described could be applied to any member of the community. "Knowing the one from the beginning" (vv. 13a; 14b) refers to Jesus, though the author maintains the close association between knowing Jesus and knowing the Father (v. 14a) from Jn 14:7-10. We have seen that Johannine christians probably came to term themselves "those who know God" during the controversy with the jews (cf. above on 2:4). The assertion of victory over the Evil One directly recalls Jesus' claim to have conquered and cast out the ruler of this world (Jn 12:31; 16:33; cf. 1 Jn 3:13; 5:18). We know from passages like Eph 6:12 that christian preachers used the imagery of the christian protected by faith in the war against the Evil One. 1 Jn may also have in mind Jesus' prayer that the Father protect from the Evil One those whom he is leaving in the world (Jn 17:15; cp. 2 Thess 3:3). Verse 14c gives the basis for victory in that context of "armour of faith," namely, "you are strong." In a typically Johannine turn, what would be the armour of faith in traditional preaching becomes "keeping the word of Jesus" (cf. 1 Jn 2:5). 1 Jn 5:4 tells us that everyone born of God conquers the world. Thus, we must assume that in this passage the author has taken the titles from the traditional household code to provide a rhetorical variation in his assurance to the community that their faith in Jesus has won forgiveness, knowledge of God, and victory over evil—just as they have always heard in Johannine preaching.

2:15-17 The World is Passing Away

> [15]Do not love the world or the things in the world. If any one loves the world, love for the Father is not in him. [16]For all that is in the world, the lust of the flesh and the lust of the eyes and the pride of life, is not of the Father but is of the world. [17]And the world passes away, and the lust of it; but he who does the will of God abides for ever.

Allusion to the impending destruction of this world is characteristic of two ways paraenesis. (Brown, [*Epistles*: 325-27], reads these verses as recast Johannine symbolism about the opposition of the world to God.) By recalling that traditional language, the author both concludes the opening exhortation and provides a transition to his claim that the opponents are "antichrists," heralds of the end-time in 2:18. The expression "the world is passing away" appears in the context of apocalyptic paraenesis in 1 Cor 7:31. There Paul encourages christians to avoid entanglement in marital relationships because the end of the world is so near, "the form of the world is passing away." The association of the transitory character of the world with desire (RSV "lust") indicates that such apocalyptic paraenesis was the source of the tradition reflected in vv. 16-17. But 1 Jn never focuses on the *nearness* of the end. Rather, the transitory character of the world stands in contrast to the eternity of the one who does the will of God. That contrast calls to mind the contrast, in Wisd 2-5, between the righteous who live forever with God and sinners who perish. "Do the will of God" is a traditional expression in jewish and christian preaching. The more usual Johannine translation of that occurs in the language about love for the Father in v. 15. If you look at Eph 5:11-16 again, you will notice that after the exhortation to "walk in the light" christians are told to be sure and have no part in the world of darkness. The same progression connects this passage to the previous one. After assuring his audience that they have won the eschatological victory, they are exhorted not to love the world. Eph vv. 15-16 also tones down the language about the nearness of the end that had characterized apocalyptic paraenesis. The warning to watch how one lives is placed in the more general context of the present as "evil times." Such an expression would originally have referred to the evil of the days just before the end of the world. Now it is used as a more general characterization of the world in which people live, just as 1 Jn is using the apocalyptic expression about the transitory nature of the world to contrast it with God and the righteous person.

The mini vice-list in v. 16 defines what love for the world is. Opposition to desire/lust appears frequently in both christian and gnostic paraenesis. "Lust of the flesh" appears in Eph 2:3 (cp. "fleshly desires" in 1 Pet 2:11; Did 1:4, both from baptismal paraenesis). Mt 5:28 might be adduced as an example of the connection between desire understood in the sexual sense and the eyes. However, we also find a saying in Wisd 14:9 which connects the eyes with greed. The final member of the chain "pride of life" explicitly refers to the boasting of a person who possesses wealth. *Bios*, translated "life" here, refers to worldly possessions (cf. 1 Jn 3:17; Mk 12:44). Brown suggests that the expression be translated "material life that inflates self-assurance." The issue would be less that of the arrogant boasting of the wealthy and successful (also see 2 Macc 9:8; 15:6; Wis 5:8) than the overconfidence that stems from such security (*Epistles*: 311-12). There is a long section of christian preaching against the passions and "friendship with the world as enmity with God" in *James* 4. It is our closest New Testament example of the kind of preaching 1 Jn 2:16-17 is summarizing. Jas 5:1-7 uses eschatological language to undergird its presentation of the transitory nature of worldly wealth and pleasure. Thus, we conclude that the minicatalogue in 1 Jn refers to three types of behavior: "lust of the flesh" to all the physical passions, not just sexual desire (note that Jas 4:1-3 ties greed as the cause of war with the desire to indulge physical passions); "lust of the eyes" refers to greed; and "pride of life" refers to the arrogant behavior charactristic of the rich and powerful.

We have seen that the language of apocalyptic paraenesis passed into gnostic circles as the complete condemnation of the body and the material world as the source of desires which trap the spirit and keep it from returning to its true divine home. Freedom from desire required rigid disciplining of the body. Some scholars have seen this passage in 1 Jn as a reflection of that gnostic mentality. We cannot agree, since it clearly stems from the tradition of baptismal paraenesis in a community which also stressed the permanent availability of forgiveness for those seeking perfection. However, such traditions of ethical preaching were easily given an anti-worldly ascetic interpretation as the gnostic evidence shows. They may have been used by 1 Jn's opponents to support their own claims for an ascetic perfection among christians.

DO NOT BE DECEIVED BY THE ANTICHRISTS
2:18-29.

>   [18]Children, it is the last hour; and as you have heard that antichrist is coming, so now many antichrists have come; therefore we know that it is the last hour. [19]They went out from us, but they were not of us; for if they had been of us, they would have continued with us; but they went out, that it might be plain that they all are not of us. [20]But you have been anointed by the Holy One, and you all know. [21]I write to you, not because you do not know the truth,but because you know it,and know that no lie is of the truth. [22]Who is the liar but he who denies that Jesus is the Christ? This is the antichrist, he who denies the

Father and the Son. [23]No one who denies the Son has the Father. He who confesses the Son has the Father also. [24]Let what you heard from the beginning abide in you. If what you heard from the beginning abides in you, then you will abide in the Son and in the Father. [25]And this is what he has promised us, eternal life.

[26]I write this to you about those who would deceive you; [27]but the anointing which you received from him abides in you, and you have no need that any one should teach you; as his anointing teaches you about everything, and is true, and is no lie, just as it has taught you, abide in him.

[28]And now, little children, abide in him, so that when he appears we may have confidence and not shrink from him in shame at his coming. [29]If you know that he is righteous, you may be sure that every one who does right is born of him.

Having established the community of believers on the basis of traditional exhortation, 1 Jn confronts the challenge threatening to divide the christian community. He begins by invoking the apocalyptic image of the antichrist, the final manifestation of evil in the last days (Mk 13:21-23, "false christs and prophets"; 2 Thess 2:3-12, the man of lawlessness, cf. Dan 11:31; Rev 13, the beast from the sea). In the usual apocalyptic scenario, such figures are cosmic or political in scope and lead people into sin or pagan belief with false signs. The author of 1 Jn assumes that his readers are familiar with the image, and he suddenly applies it in the plural to the christian opponents who are leading people away from the traditional teaching. Notice that there are no "signs and wonders" associated with the people to whom he is referring. In this respect 1 Jn is quite unusual. Even when the same imagery is used in gnostic texts of the 2nd century, it still retains the traditional cluster of associations. *Paraphrase of Shem* predicts the coming of a demonic figure (given the use of ancient Near Eastern water-monster mythology this figure is closest to Rev 13), who will lead people away from the true gnosis (CG VII *1* 43,28-45,31; *NHLE*:

326f). Gnostics can even epitomize their suppression by orthodox authorities by speaking of an end-time in which a false god, complete with signs and wonders, will arise and pervert the teaching of the gospel (*Concept of Our Great Power* CG VI *4* 44,13-46,5; *NHLE*: 288). 1 Jn makes no attempt to impose that sort of cosmic imagery on the group he is opposing. Therefore, we do not accept the claim made by some interpreters that his use of "antichrist" shows his eschatology to be more primitive than that of the fourth evangelist. As in the previous passage, he simply takes over apocalyptic language to intensify the picture of the seriousness of the opposition; he is not interested in apocalyptic preaching about the impending end. Note, for example, he does not go on to predict the apocalyptic destruction of his opponents, something even the later gnostic writings do!

Verse 19 makes it clear that the people in question were not new converts but established members of the community. It is also clear that their separation was not the result of a formal excommunication such as we know was the penalty for severe lapses from the essene rule and was prescribed by Paul in a severe case of immorality (1 Cor 5:3-5). The author's concern to assure his audience that these people are not really "from us" (v.19c) and to warn them against being led astray by their teaching (v.26) shows that they have not established a completely independent sect. If the opponents claim to be continuing the Johannine *koinonia*, then their separation from the truth might not appear evident to the audience. The apocalyptic images draw the boundaries between the two groups in the sharpest possible terms. Brown suggests that the author may also have had the Johannine description of Judas' betrayal of Jesus in mind as the archtype for the opponents (6:70-71; 13:2, 27, 30; *Epistles*: 367 n. 14).

However, this section does not make clear the nature of their teaching. Commentators have tried to find forms of gnostic christology to fit v.22 "deny Jesus is the Christ." But while it is true that many gnostic christologies distinguish the heavenly, spiritual part of the revealer, the immortal man, Son, or Son of Man, from his bodily part, they do so in order to free the divine from any involvement with sinfulness, suffering or death. They frequently give explanations of the virgin birth of Jesus in order to show him as a worthy vessel for the divine spirit (cf. *Tripartite Tractate* CG I *5* 115,3-116,30, *NHLE*: 87f, here even the apostles have a special origin; *Gospel of Philip* CG II *3* 55, 23-36; 71,13-15, *NHLE*: 134; 143; *Second Apocalypse of James* CG V *4* 50,8-51,13, *NHLE*: 251; *Testimony of Truth* CG IX *3* 30,18-31,5, *NHLE*: 407, in this ascetic work Jesus must be pure and undefiled by passions). The heavenly revealer may even take the crucified Jesus up to his dwelling with the Father (*Trimorphic Protennoia* CG XIII *1* 50,12-15, *NHLE*: 470). There is no known gnostic christology that really fits the slogan. We suggest that v.22 never was intended to represent the opposing point of view. The language of vv.22-23 is very close to that which emerged from the polemic with judaism in which the distinctive theological language of the Johannine gospel developed. At that time, people were denying the messiahship of Jesus, and much of the controversy swirled around the Johannine insight that the Son is the only true revelation of the Father. The gospel continuously insists that no one can claim to accept or believe in God—as the jewish teachers did—without accepting Jesus (5:23; 8:19; 12:44f; 14:9; 15:23; 16:3; 17:3). Our author is assimilating the present crisis to the symbols developed in the past one in which many of the members of the community had suffered persecution (15:23; 16:3, the persecution is associated with the slogan of the identity of Son and Father). His opponents would certainly reject any connection with those who had denied Christ rather than suffer persecution. Brown acknowledges that the opponents would not have felt their confession of Jesus to be in error, but he reconstructs a christological division to account for all the accusations of denial in which the opponents focus on the preexistent word as Christ rather than acknowledging the life of Jesus as Incarnate Word. He then attaches the ethical problems, which have so far dominated the letter, to a presumed indifference to the ethical importance of "the way Jesus walked" for Christians (*Epistles*: 368).

We have already mentioned that the symbol of the paraclete developed as part of the authority of christian claims for Jesus when pitted against jewish opposition (see above on 2:1f). Jn 14 shows paraclete language to be convertible with that about the spirit and the indwelling of Father and Son. 1 Jn is evoking these images. It is likely that "spirit" or "anointing" was the more usual way of speaking about the activity of the divine within the community. As in the gospel, possession of the spirit belongs to the whole community. 1 Jn does not develop a doctrine of some spirit-endowed official within the community to hand on and safeguard the tradition. The spirit as anointing guides the community as a whole to faithful witness to the teaching "from the beginning." Some commentators think that he has picked the term "anointing" in opposition to its use among gnostics, but it was more likely the way in which Johannine christians commonly supported their claims to true religious insight (vv.20f; 26f). It may also have had associations with baptismal initiation (see Brown's discussion of the author's concern to recall that language, [*Epistles*: 370-71]). Just as the paraclete in Jn 14 is to lead the community to true understanding of Jesus' teaching and may be considered identical with the indwelling Father and Son (Jn 14:16f; 26), so 1 Jn is convinced that testimony to what has been from the beginning within the community anointed by the spirit, or alternatively, the community which remains in unity with Father and Son, is sufficient to counter false teaching. The apparent denial of the need for any human teachers in the Christian community sets this passage apart from the concern for a legitimate teaching authority to counter such dissent that we find elsewhere in the NT (see Brown, *Epistles*: 374-76).

The apocalyptic language of v.18 returns in vv.28-29. The author has constructed his initial response to the opponents in two parallel sections vv.20-25//26-29. Both begin by asserting the effectiveness of testimony within the "anointed" community against false teaching, and then conclude with an eschatological promise to those who *remain in* that community. (For this reason, we have not followed the practice of most commentators and attached vv.28-29 to the beginning of chapter 3, although the reformulated tradition in v.29 does seem to have been designed as a bridge to the next section of the epistle.) Verse 25 uses typically Johannine language to promise the believer eternal life. Like v.18, vv.28f return to apocalyptic images. The faithful believer can be confident that he or she will not be shamed at the judgment (v.28). Verse 29 takes a traditional assertion, the righteousness of God demands that one do righteousness to be saved and casts it in Johannine language, the one who does righteousness is born of God. The expression "born of God" provides a bridge to the next section, which will return to ethical instruction. Statements about the conditions of divine begetting occur throughout the second half of the letter (2:29; 3:9; 4:7; 5:1, 5, 18). 1 Jn 5:1 speaks of belief as the condition for divine begetting (cp. Jn 1:12). The other passages refer to the way in which a person lives, e.g. does not sin (3:9); loves (4:7). The Johannine tradition of believers as "begotten of" (children of) God coupled with the way of life to which that leads is to provide assurance in the judgment.

THE CHILDREN OF GOD.
3:1-10.

> **3** See what love the Father has given us, that we should be called children of God; and so we are. The reason why the world does not know us is that it did not know him. ²Beloved, we are God's children now; it does not yet appear what we shall be, but we know that when he appears we shall be like him, for we shall see him as he is. ³And every one who thus hopes in him purifies himself as he is pure.
>
> ⁴Every one who commits sin is guilty of lawlessness; sin is lawlessness. ⁵You know that he appeared to take away sins, and in him there is no sin. ⁶No one who abides

in him sins; no one who sins has either seen him or known him. ⁷Little children, let no one deceive you. He who does right is righteous, as he is righteous. ⁸He who commits sin is of the devil; for the devil has sinned from the beginning. The reason the Son of God appeared was to destroy the works of the devil. ⁹No one born of God commits sin; for God's nature abides in him, and he cannot sin because he is born of God. ¹⁰By this it may be seen who are the children of God, and who are the children of the devil; whoever does not do right is not of God, nor he who does not love his brother.

1 Jn 2:29 provided the transition to this section by speaking of those who do righteousness as God is righteous as being "born of God" and confident of their salvation. Chapter 3 picks up these themes. The children of God are distinguished from the children of the devil. Then, at the end of the chapter, it returns to the confidence possessed by the community in which the spirit of God dwells. This section provides some of the basis for that confidence, since the christian community possesses righteousness and sinlessness. There is little that is new in this section of 1 Jn. The author picks up the themes of traditional paraenesis to reinforce the conviction and allegiance of the members of his audience. He seeks to lay bare the essential distinction between them and the opponents whom he wishes to show are "not of us." As in the previous section, one method of making this distinction is to allude to the language of the gospel in such a way as to identify the present opponents with those of the gospel.

The expression "children of God" seems to have been one of the community's traditional self-designations. (For the OT background of the expression "sons of God" to speak of those who are united in a covenant relationship with God, see Brown, *Epistles*, 389-90.) The expression "children" occurs in close proximity with another favorite, "born of God," which Jn 3:5 suggests was associated with baptismal initiation into the community (cf. born in 1 Jn 2:29;

3:9; 5:1; 5:18; children in 3:1,2,10; 5:2). Judaism had already developed the image of the righteous person as "Son of God." It occurs in Wisd 2:18 and 5:5, a passage which we have already connected with Johannine paraenesis in 2:16f. The righteousness brought by Jesus led christians to claim to be "sons of God." Rom 8:12-25 may well represent the kind of christian preaching that we find here cast into Johannine language. Romans uses both "children" and "sons" for the new status of christians. That status derives from the fact that the spirit of God enables christians to live a new life "not according to the flesh"; to address God as Father, and to hope and long for the future revelation of glory in which they will receive full adoption as sons of God. 1 Jn is without the cosmic imagery of a transformed creation—unless one reads "dissolving the works of the devil" in those terms. But the passage expresses similar sentiments. Christians stand in a special relationship to God now as a result of what Christ has already done; they live a renewed life which is not subject to sin, but at the same time, the salvation which he has made possible is not completed in the present. Christians still hope for the future conformity to Christ and for the revelation of his true glory—which for the Johannine tradition is that of the exalted Christ with his Father (17:1,5,24).

This passage stresses the sinlessness of the life of the children of God. Many interpreters think these claims to be in conflict with the warning against supposing oneself to be sinless in 1:6,8 and the doctrine of forgiveness 2:1f; (so Brown, *Epistles*, 389-90). They wonder how the author differs from his opponents. Solutions to the dilemma frequently hypothesize a progressive understanding of perfection in 1 Jn—implied, it is claimed, by the eschatological reservation in v.2. This progressive doctrine is contrasted with the false reading of gnosticism as teaching that the gnostic cannot sin. We understand the author to be presenting a consistent picture of sin and perfection. The admonitions in chapter 1 derived from the baptismal tradition. The neophyte cannot enter the community without recognizing his or her need for the forgiveness made available in Christ. Chapter 2 distinguishes the possible sinfulness of the individual christian from the forgiveness which is always available. Here the author is primarily interested in the holiness and righteousness of the community in order to encourage his audience not to "go out from us." If the opponents were, as we have suggested, demanding a high degree of individual perfection, then the author must show that christians do possess the perfection they are accused of lacking. He is no more interested in the sins of a particular individual at this point than Paul was when he spoke of "walking according to the spirit" in Rom 8.

The community in which the spirit of God dwells can be said to possess perfection despite the transgressions of individuals. This combination emerges clearly among the essenes, who have elaborate legislation for members who mar the holiness and purity of the community, but who can also see the whole community as embodying the righteousness and perfection of God. What 1 Jn has refused to do is to adopt an option for holiness in which the community would follow a rigid code and exclude members who do not conform. He understands the forgiveness won by Jesus as making that approach unnecessary. At the same time, it is easy to see that the language about righteousness and purity derived from apocalyptic preaching could lead some christians to insist that individuals should embody that purity and perhaps even seek to dissociate themselves from those who did not do so. The author is insisting on the community as the place in which one finds perfection. He is not putting forth a philosophical doctrine of a soul purified from passions. (See Philo *de fug* cxviv for such a psychological approach: the soul is incapable of sin as long as the divine word is within.)

Some interpreters claim that v.9 makes a community-based interpretation of the Johannine understanding of perfection impossible, because it expands the "born from God" language with the claim that those in whom God's seed dwells cannot sin. (RSV misleadingly translates "seed" as "nature" and has thus not only obscured the exegetical background of the passage but introduced a philosophical term which weights the interpretation of the passage in the direction of "sinless essence.") A brief look at some of the sources of the "seed" metaphor will explain its presence here. (Brown, *Epistles*: 408-411). Within the epistle itself, you may notice that the previous verse refers back to the controversy with the jews in Jn 8. That controversy was introduced by their claim to be "seed of Abraham" and free. Jesus countered it by insisting that they do not do the righteousness characteristic of true sons of God since they reject his testimony and seek to kill him. We may suggest, then, that the "seed of God" image is another example of community language developed to distinguish christians from their jewish opposition. Philo (*vit. mos.* i, 279) speaks of the people of Israel as from a divine seed, which suggests that the christian title may have had jewish roots. Later the gnostics speak of themselves as "seed of Seth," the true sons of Adam as opposed to others derived from Cain or perhaps even to jews who also claimed descent from Seth. Both jewish and gnostic traditions have derived the "seed" metaphor from Genesis accounts of the true people of God. It is a group designation not an individual one. 1 Jn is about to appeal to Genesis explicitly when he introduces the Cain story in 3:12. The previous allusion to Jn 8 in combination with an explicit one to Genesis, to Cain as an example of "sin from the beginning," probably led to the introduction of the seed metaphor here. There is no reason to assume that 1 Jn has taken over the gnostic technical term being used by his opponents. We find other examples of Johannine self-designations, which we have already suggested were part of the community tradition, in verse 6 (know/see God).

The previous passage used apocalyptic images to castigate the author's opponents. Many expressions in this section have a similar ring. Apocalyptic preaching commonly divided humanity into two groups, the righteous and the wicked (sons of light and sons of darkness, or of Beliar). Sin is frequently defined as lawlessness (v.4; cf. Ps 32:1; Jer 31:34; Rom 4:7; Heb 10:17; 2 Thess 2:8 antichrist=man of lawlessness). It was also common to emphasize the deception that would characterize the last days. People would be led astray from righteousness into sin as in the traditional phrasing of v.7 (contrast the use of deceive in a doctrinal sense in 2:26).

Verse 8 allows the author to complete his identification of the two groups, using images derived from the fourth gospel. In the controversy with the jews in Jn 8, those who reject Jesus are called children of the devil, who show the passions of their father—especially, since they seek to kill Jesus—his being a murderer from the beginning (8:44). Here he is referred to as a "sinner from the beginning," but "murderer" is behind the more general "sinner." The author is about to introduce murder as the prime example of hating one's brother. Division of humanity into righteous, pure, over against sinners (vv.3,10) is common apocalyptic preaching. The author marks the transition between such traditional language and the central claim of the Johannine community when he makes "love for the brethren" the criterion for dividing the two groups (v.10b).

We see from this analysis of the author's language that he is not describing the spiritual state of individuals but the christian community as the true, righteous people of God. The claim in v.8 that Jesus appeared to "destroy the works of the devil" shows that he has the cosmic defeat of the power of evil in mind when he speaks of Jesus taking away sins (v.5) not simply particular sins of individuals. It is a fundamental conviction of Johannine theology that Jesus' coming accomplished the victory over evil which had been the object of so much apocalyptic preaching. He has established the community whose righteousness and holiness may be described in terms of God's dwelling with his people. We have seen 1 Jn refer to both God and Jesus with the expression "he is righteous" (2:29). Here traditional attributes of God, holiness and righteousness, refer both to the Father (vv.3 & 7) and to the Son, who is called "sinless" in v.5—though not in terms of his sacrificial death but as an indication of his essential identity with the Father.

In chapters 1 & 2, the author alternated the light metaphor between God and Jesus; using it in both instances as paraenesis for how christians should "walk." He seems to be doing the same thing in this passage, since his primary focus is on the relationship between the christian and God. The christian is "begotten from Him." Thus we should not reduce the language of vv.3,5, & 7 to a doctrine of imitating virtues of Jesus. The author wishes to show that the community mirrors the perfection of its father. Perhaps he insists on the present reality of their status as children of God (v.2a) in response to the kind of christian apocalyptic preaching which deferred full adoption as sons to the future (e.g. Rom 8:14,19; Gal 3:26; 4:6f). The rest of this verse expresses the eschatological conviction that Jesus' full reality has yet to be seen. Although we cannot be certain of what the future of the believer will be like, we can be certain that it will be like the glorified state of Jesus (cf. Jn 17:24). Paul has a similar eschatological reservation when describing the resurrection of christians (Rom 8:29; 1 Cor 15:50f; 2 Cor 3:18). 1 Jn's reservation is not a way of saying that a person becomes progressively like Christ—a concept not introduced until christians began to assimilate the terminology of philosophical education. The reservation preserves the "in between" status of christian life without a heavy investment in an apocalyptic timetable about the impending end of the world. Though christians truly are children of God, their divine sonship is not the completion of the divine act of salvation. Verse 1 applies the contrast between their knowledge of the Father and the world's failure to acknowledge Jesus and hence those he sends (cp. Jn 15:18f,23; 16:3)—originally an answer to the puzzles of persecution—to the permanent life of the community (cf. Jn 17:15f). At the same time, the whole section implies that the opponents are to be associated with "the world" and "the children of the devil," and implies that their preaching is as much a threat and rejection of Jesus and the Father as was the earlier persecution. This section reminds the community of what they had learned when they were initiated/baptized. (See the parallels to 1 Pet 1:3,13,18-23; 2:9; and Tit 2:11-14; 3:4-7 in Brown [*Epistles*: 432-34], these show that common themes of such paraenesis are being used here.

LOVE THE BRETHREN.
3:11-18.

> [11]For this is the message which you have heard from the beginning, that we should love one another, [12]and not be like Cain who was of the evil one and murdered his brother. And why did he murder him? Because his own deeds were evil and his brother's righteous. [13]Do not wonder, brethren, that the world hates you. [14]We know that we have passed out of death into life, because we love the brethren. He who does not love remains in death. [15]Any one who hates his brother is a murderer, and you know that no murderer has eternal life abiding in him. [16]By this we know love, that he laid down his life for us; and we ought to lay down our lives for the brethren. [17]But if any one has the world's goods and sees his brother in need, yet closes his heart against him, how does God's love abide in him? [18]Little children, let us not love in word or speech but in deed and in truth.

1 Jn returns to the teaching on love which had been established in the traditional paraenesis of 2:7-11. He continues the imagery from Jn 8 and the use of "world" as symbolic of all that is hostile to God's revelation as means of condemning the opponents. The story of Cain becomes an example of the most radical manner of hating a brother, murder. "Hatred of the brethren" does not refer to any particular ethical deviation of the author's opponents. The author is marshalling the resources of the community's tradition to reassure his audience. The opening formula is almost identical with 1:5. There the confession "God is light" introduced baptismal paraenesis. Here "love one another" is announced as *the message*; the teaching which

the Johannine community saw as its very foundation (see above on 2:7-11).

Jude 11 refers to evil people as walking in the way of Cain. Abel is an example of righteousness and faith in Heb 11:4. A late gnostic work, *Valentinian Exposition*, preserves an old jewish tradition in which Cain and Abel represent the twofold division of humanity. Cain is inspired by the devil (the "murderer from the beginning" in Jn 8) when he murders his brother (CG XI *2* 38,24-33). Such a tradition may underlie Jn 8 and the author's selection of the Cain story here. The Johannine community may have used Cain as an example of the murderous intentions of the world during the persecution. They may even have spoken of the Jews as "seed of Cain" just as Jn 8 denies them the appellation "seed of Abraham." Hebrews shows that tradition associated righteousness with Abel as is the case here [see further examples in Brown, *Epistles*: 442-43].

"Hatred by the world," which now appears frequently as an oblique reference to the opponents, is Johannine language from the earlier conflict (Jn 15:18f; 17:14). Verses 14-15 interpret the Cain story in terms of the love command. The expression "we have passed from death to life" comes from Jn 5:24. There it distinguishes those who believe in Jesus from those who do not; here, it distinguishes true christians from the opponents, who also claim to be christians.

The meaning of the love commandment is illustrated by the example of Jesus laying down his life (Jn 10:11,15, for his sheep; 15:13, for his "friends"). Though christians are encouraged to follow a similar example, it is clear that members of the Johannine community are no longer threatened with death for their faith. Verse 17 draws a more practical conclusion, which is typical early christian preaching (see Jas 2:14-17): one must be willing to share one's wealth with christians in need. The expression "world" in this verse refers to the transitory character of those material possessions for which people competed and in which they displayed such pride (see above on 2:16). Such preaching typically included the demand to express one's belief in deeds and not just words (v.18; cp. Jas 1:22; 2:15f; Mt 7:21).

OUR CONFIDENCE BEFORE GOD.
3:19-24.

> [19]By this we shall know that we are of the truth, and reassure our hearts before him [20]whenever our hearts condemn us; for God is greater than our hearts, and he knows everything. [21]Beloved, if our hearts do not condemn us, we have confidence before God; [22]and we receive from him whatever we ask, because we keep his commandments and do what pleases him. [23]And this is his commandment, that we should believe in the name of his Son Jesus Christ and love one another, just as he has commanded us. [24]All who keep his commandments abide in him, and he in them. And by this we know that he abides in us, by the Spirit which he has given us.

Confidence in their salvation was a key issue in the community (cp. 2:28f). This section of 1 Jn founds that confidence on the Johannine understanding of the true community of those who love each other as the abiding place of the spirit of God. For those who remain in that community, God guarantees salvation even against the accusations of one's own heart (vv. 19-20). That claim reflects the gospel's view that judgment occurs when one either accepts or rejects Jesus. The language of this section is so much less that of traditional early christian and Johannine preaching that it may well reflect the type of debate immediately affecting the community.

1 Jn 2:28-29 referred to the believer's confidence in the face of future judgment. Here the author goes further: even now the christian's heart should not condemn him (v.21). The fourth gospel uses the word translated "confidence" only in connection with the true community. In 16:25,29, Jesus now speaks "openly" with his disciples about the Father. The same gospel passage associates that speaking

with the fact that the disciples can now approach the Father in prayer directly, since he loves those who believe in Jesus (Jn 16:26f; cf. 1 Jn 5:14; Jn 14:13f; 15:7; Mk 11:24 par). 1 Jn usually picks up language from the gospel that emphasizes the direct relationship between the christian and God as in the sayings on prayer in Jn 16 rather than that which implies some mediation by Jesus as in Jn 14. He wishes to found the christian's confidence on the new relationship with the Father. This relationship presupposes keeping his commandments (see also 1 Jn 2:3,4; 5:2f; 2 Jn 6; Jn 15:10, 15,21). The alternative expression "do what is pleasing to him" is typical paraenetic language (cf. Jn 8:29; Heb 13:21). Verse 23 summarizes "commandments" as belief in the name of His son and loving one another. We have seen the latter frequently as the epitome of Johannine paraenesis. This is the first time belief in Jesus appears. It will recur in future condemnations of the opponents (4:16; 5:1,20). The requirement of belief refers us back to similar demands in the fourth gospel where it is the guarantee of eternal life, of having passed through the judgment (Jn 5:24; 1 Jn 4:13; 5:5?). Thus, the author is still using the language of the gospel to make his case for the confidence he wishes to instill in his audience.

The concluding verses return to the theme of the indwelling of God with those who keep his commandments, but they also introduce a new motif in order to make the transition to the new section: God's indwelling is verified by the presence of the spirit in the community (3:24 = 4:13). The spirit's role is crucial to the Johannine understanding of the community as witness to the truth about Jesus as was already suggested in the discussion of anointing in 2:26f. It returns as guarantor of their teaching in the next section. Late jewish eschatology associated the presence of the spirit of God in the community with the new age. Its presence was felt to be anticipated in eschatological communities such as we find at Qumran (e.g. 1 QH 12.12; 13.19) and in early christianity (e.g. 1 Thess 4:8; Rom 5:5). The Johannine tradition seems to have moved beyond understanding the presence of the spirit as an indication of the elect community on the verge of the messianic age, to using images of the presence of the spirit, God or Jesus as guaranteeing its ongoing life and testimony to Jesus as the one sent by God.

One should not think from this passage in 1 Jn that members of the community were all afflicted by "guilt" in the modern psychological sense, or that they were suffering from the demands of an impossible ethic embodied in the love command as some interpreters have suggested. The crisis faced by the author has not been raised by the pastoral problem of dealing with individual "guilt feelings." It has been raised by those who questioned the Johannine understanding of salvation. The evidences which the author is suggesting to guarantee their certainty of salvation do not require the individual to feel some internal verification or manifestation of the spirit. They ask whether or not he or she belongs to the community in which the spirit of God dwells, to the community which is characterized by its belief in Jesus and its practice of brotherly love. That practice is not defined in psychological terms. An individual is not asked how he feels about his brother but whether he has helped a brother in need when he had the means to do so. This practical demand is rhetorically situated to come as something of a relief—following as it does the suggestion that one should be willing to die for a brother! Even if his heart should condemn him (and the author is not saying that it does), then God will guarantee his salvation.

TEST THE SPIRITS.
4:1-6.

> **4** Beloved, do not believe every spirit, but test the spirits to see whether they are of God; for many false prophets have gone out into the world. [2]By this you know the Spirit of God: every spirit which confesses that Jesus Christ has come in the flesh is of God, [3]and every spirit which does not confess Jesus is not of God. This is the spirit of antichrist, of which you heard that it was coming,

and now it is in the world already. ⁴Little children, you are of God, and have overcome them; for he who is in you is greater than he who is in the world. ⁵They are of the world, therefore what they say is of the world, and the world listens to them. ⁶We are of God. Whoever knows God listens to us, and he who is not of God does not listen to us. By this we know the spirit of truth and the spirit of error.

The author returns to direct attack on his opponents by once again invoking the ominous language of apocalyptic preaching. Since he is still reading the present situation in terms of past crises, we must continue to sift through his rhetoric very carefully. The only certain indications 1 Jn has given of the opponents' doctrine are that they have denied the Johannine understanding of the death of Jesus as atonement for the sins of christians and undermined the community's confidence in their own salvation. In response, he has taken great pains to show that the community of those who love one another has God present with it in such a way as to establish both perfection and forgiveness. The message of chapter 4 largely reformulates these earlier themes. Chapter 3 began by distinguishing two groups of "children," those of God and those of the devil. This chapter begins by distinguishing two spirits, truth and error. A doctrine of "two spirits" was commonly associated with two-ways paraenesis (see Brown, *Epistles*: 487) in which it accounts for good and evil people. The author probably derived it from such preaching. But he is not using it to make ethical distinctions in this passage; it accounts for the two types of christian teaching.

This section forms a neat rhetorical unity: the opening demand for distinguishing spirits concludes with the established separation of the two spirits at the end. That separation is accomplished by using the language of apocalyptic and Johannine dualism to present the audience with two clearly distinguished sides:

"us"	"them"
spirit of God (v.1)	spirit of antichrist (v.3)
spirit of God (v.1)	false prophets (v.1)
of God (v.4)	of the world (v.5)
confess Jesus Christ came in the flesh (v.2)	deny Jesus (v.3)
recognized by those who "know God" (v.6)	listened to by the world (v.5)
spirit of truth (v.6)	spirit of error (v.6)

With the exception of the confession in v.2, all the other assertions here have parallels either in apocalyptic preaching or in the Johannine reformulation of that language. The fourth gospel assured persecuted christians that although the religious authorities opposed them, they had the truth about Jesus. Their persecution is to be expected from a world which has rejected Jesus and his word (Jn 17:14). They possess the "spirit of truth" to guarantee their teaching (Jn 14:17,26; 16:13; and see the discussion of 1 Jn 2:20-22). Jn 17:25 contrasts Jesus who "knows the Father" and the disciples who "know that Jesus is sent from Him" with the world which does not know God. "Those who know God" (v.6) became one of the self-designations of Johannine christians (see above on 1 Jn 2:4). As in 1 Jn 2:18, apocalyptic predictions about antichrist and false prophecy are applied to the opponents. But rather than look toward future destruction of evil people, the Johannine tradition always emphasized the present victory of Jesus (and through him the christian) over evil or "the world." Now that he has cast the opponents in the negative role of "the world," the author may apply that victory language to his audience's relationship with them: God (or his spirit) is greater than the world (v.4; cp. Jn 17:14-16, Jesus asks the Father to protect his followers, who do not belong to the world, from the evil one).

The real exegetical problem in this section is the confession mentioned in v.2 and the associated testing of spirits. That confession reappears in 2 Jn 7 as a point about which the addressees might be deceived by false teachers. Notice that in v.3 the opponents are accused simply of denying Jesus. (The RSV has accepted a manuscript reading "do not confess" rather than the *luein*, lit. dissolve, destroy, preferred by most commentators. See Brown, *Epistles*: 494-96. Brown's "negate the importance of" seems to us too interpretive a translation; Schnackenburg suggests "deny," while Bultmann has opted for a somewhat stronger "annul Jesus.") We have seen that it is a standard rhetorical tactic of the author to associate his opponents with those who in the earlier crisis really did deny the messiahship of Jesus or his being Son of God. This traditional confession is used in all the christological assertions in the epistles (1 Jn 2:22; 4:15; 5:1,5) except this passage and 2 Jn 7. We also know (e.g. Jn 17:25) that Jesus as "one sent from God" is a traditional christological slogan in Johannine circles. In order to be members of the community, 1 Jn's opponents must have accepted all these slogans even if the author does try to insinuate that they do not. Is the formulation in v.2 another traditional slogan from that earlier controversy? Or has the author taken a traditional confession "Jesus is the one sent from (coming from) God" and revised it to fit the new situation by adding "in the flesh"? In either case, one cannot reconstruct a christology of the opponents on the basis of this slogan.

Gnostic evidence does not support the kind of docetism frequently adduced for this passage. Brown agrees that the opponents did not deny the physical reality of Jesus' humanity. He sugests that they held the view that what Jesus did in his earthly life had no connection to salvation (*Epistles*: 505). It seems more likely that christology was not the real issue at all. 1 Jn has been concerned all along with problems of soteriology. The confidence of christians in salvation and forgiveness based on the atoning death of Jesus has been shaken (1:7; 2:2; 3:5; 4:10; 5:6). The author may have updated an old slogan by adding "in flesh," but we cannot be sure whether his opponents would have been forced to reject that modification or not.

Commentators usually try to locate the "testing of spirits" within the context of early christian problems about testing, controlling, or legitimating prophetic or ecstatic phenomena within the life of the community. They rightly point out that our author shows no evidence of having to deal with the kind of ecstatic prophecy mentioned in 2 Thess 5:19f or 1 Cor 12:3-10, for example (see Brown *Epistles*: 506). Nor does he seem concerned with wandering preachers or wonder-workers who might preside over liturgical celebrations as in Did 11, either. We can perhaps gain some insight into what the author has in mind in v.2, if we begin with Houlden's suggestion (p. 108) that "confess" implies a liturgical context. Or, at least, a communal assembly of some sort. Oaths before the assembly played an important role in greek legal history. Development of courts and legal proceedings lessened the role played by such formal oaths, but one might still try to cut short a lengthly legal proceeding by demanding that one's opponent take an oath as to the facts of the case. Communities which relied solely on oral procedures for settling disputes and making agreements continued to place great weight on the formal oath taken before the assembly. It could even be that "christological slogans" played a role in the forensic proceedings to which christians had been subject during the persecution (see the way in which the Pharisees interrogate the blind man as to "who Jesus is" in Jn 9 for an example). The role that such slogans have in the language of the Johannine community suggests that initiation of new members may have been accompanied by pronouncing such confessions. Thus, we suggest that "testing the spirits" may be intended to have legal overtones: a person might be asked to "take an oath" in the presence of the community. The author may have devised the slogan in v.2 (and 2 Jn 7) as a model for use in such proceedings; as a way of testing those people whom he says are not really christians (2:19) and whose teaching should not be accepted.

The expression "the world listens to them" coupled with the "many" in 2 Jn 7 suggests to some interpreters that the author's tests are not working. The opponents are more successful as far as numbers of adherents are concerned (Brown, *Epistles*: 507). Apocalyptic rhetoric typically speaks of "many" being led astray. Verse 5 is just another of the author's appeals to the rhetoric of the fourth gospel to identify the opponents with the "unbelieving jews" (who are "from the world," Jn 8:23).

LOVE IN THE CHRISTIAN COMMUNITY.
4:7-16a.

> [7]Beloved, let us love one another; for love is of God, and he who loves is born of God and knows God. [8]He who does not love does not know God; for God is love. [9]In this the love of God was made manifest among us, that God sent his only Son into the world, so that we might live through him. [10]In this is love, not that we loved God but that he loved us and sent his Son to be the expiation for our sins. [11]Beloved, if God so loved us, we also ought to love one another. [12]No man has ever seen God; if we love one another, God abides in us and his love is perfected in us.
>
> [13]By this we know that we abide in him and he in us, because he has given us of his own Spirit. [14]And we have seen and testify that the Father has sent his Son as the Savior of the world. [15]Whoever confesses that Jesus is the Son of God, God abides in him, and he in God. [16]So we know and believe the love God has for us.

We have chosen (with the Bible Society Greek New Testament) to divide verse 16, though the whole could belong to this section, and to take 16b "God is love" as the introduction to the next section (by analogy with 1:5). This whole part of 1 Jn is made up of short units which refer to tradition already known to the readers. It continues the author's policy of grounding the community and its tradition in its relationship to God himself. After expounding the principle "God is love" in vv. 7-10, the author applies it to the community in vv. 11-16a.

Verses 7-8 repeat a familiar point. Knowledge and perfection of divine love are tied to keeping the commandment, namely, loving one another (e.g. 2:4f). These verses combine the perception that love is the activity which characterizes full divine activity with the theme from 2:29 in which a person whose life corresponds with the pattern set by God can be spoken of as "begotten by God." The first section of 1 Jn made similar use of "God is light" to exhort christians to "walk in light." These examples point to an important feature of 1 Jn's use of divine attributes. They are not abstract statements about the nature of deity such as one might find in a philosophy of religion. Light, righteousness, love (and the "pure" and "sinless" applied to Jesus in 3:3,5, as well), are all derived from God's saving activity on behalf of humanity. The Johannine tradition sees that activity focused in Jesus, who is the light in which christians walk (1 Jn 2:8b); is righteous (3:7b), and is the revelation of the love of God (v.9; cp. Jn 3:16-18) and the source of their life (v.9; also 1:2; Jn 1:4; 3:16; 5:21b). Johannine tradition characteristically speaks of Jesus as "only begotten son" (cp. Jn 1:14-18; 3:16-18). In the fourth gospel, it served to emphasize the unique relationship between Jesus and God so as to make him the only source of revelation about the Father. Verse 10 expands verse 9, making it clear that the author is not speaking about love of God as some human achievement. The "we ought to love one another" is not a way of compelling a response from God, but itself derives from the action God has taken on our behalf. 1 Jn thus expresses a fundamental insight of the covenant theology of the Old Testament as it had been handed on in christianity: God takes the initiative in reconciling a sinful humanity to himself (e.g. Rom 3:21-25; 8:32,39; see Schnackenburg: 233-35). Rom 3:21-25 ties that terminology with the sacrificial death of Jesus. 1 Jn, perhaps in opposition to his opponents, also emphasizes the death of Jesus as reconciling sacrifice.

The move from the love of God shown in the death of Jesus (v.10) to paraenesis (v.11) parallels the injunction of 3:16. Verse 12 draws further consequences for christian life from another favorite Johannine phrase about God, "no one has seen him." In the fourth gospel, expressions like "no one has seen God except the Son who makes him known" (1:18; 3:13, only Jesus has ascended to heaven, 5:37, Jesus' opponents have never seen the Father, 6:46) play an important role in the conflict with the jews. Contrary to jewish claims that Jesus is leading people astray, Moses, Abraham and other prophets and visionaries whom their tradition claims have seen God, have not done so. Only Jesus has seen and can reveal the Father. Both Moses (5:45) and Abraham (8:56) testify to him. This tradition is the one to which the author now appeals. 1 Jn is appealing to a traditional slogan, used to establish Jesus as the sole source of religious truth. He will draw an ethical conclusion from that slogan just as he has been doing with the statements about other divine attributes. God may be unseen by men, but his presence in the community is not. God abides with those who love one another. 1 Jn 2:5 made a parallel assertion: God's love for humanity is perfected in the one who keeps his word. There as here, that love is tied to confidence in abiding with God.

Verses 13-16 present other signs of the community's relationship with God. 1 Jn 4:13 repeats 3:24b—the phrase must have been a well-known formula. The introduction to v.14 recalls 1:1-4. It is followed by two traditional claims about Jesus. God has sent his son, a persistent theme in the gospel (e.g. 3:17, above v.10), and Jesus is savior of the world (Jn 4:46, where it shows the universality of Jesus' mission). "Jesus is Son of God" was also an important confessional formula in the community (cf. 1 Jn 5:5). Verse 15b expands the Son of God title with the abiding language so typical of the Johannine way of referring to the presence of God in the community. This expansion is not a new development in the tradition. Jn 14:10 explains that the works Jesus has done are from the Father abiding in him. Therefore, we assume that vv.14-15 are repeating the community's traditional understanding of the relationship between Jesus and the Father, which is the basis for his revelation of the Father's love. Verse 16a forms an *inclusio* with v.11: the community is convinced of God's love.

GOD'S LOVE AS OUR CONFIDENCE.
4:16b-21.

> God is love, and he who abides in love abides in God, and God abides in him. [17]In this is love perfected with us, that we may have confidence for the day of judgment, because as he is so are we in this world. [18]There is no fear in love, but perfect love casts out fear. For fear has to do with punishment, and he who fears is not perfected in love. [19]We love, because he first loved us. [20]If any one says, "I love God," and hates his brother, he is a liar; for he who does not love his brother whom he has seen, cannot love God whom he has not seen. [21]And this commandment we have from him, that he who loves God should love his brother also.

The second "God is love" (16b; cf. 8b) returns to the theme of christian confidence. It provides the most radical grounding of that confidence yet—though one not materially different from the previous two. 1 Jn 2:28 grounded confidence in the judgment in the justice of God toward those who also do righteousness. The most traditional of the three passages, it could well derive from jewish teaching. In 3:21-24, confidence in prayer is founded on the direct relationship to the Father enjoyed by those who believe in Jesus, keep his command of love, and to whom the Father has given his spirit. Here, God's action in showing his love is the basis for confidence and for the love christians are to show one another. Verse 16b repeats the themes of 3:24 and 4:13,15. Everything 1 Jn has been saying about Jesus' advocacy and the resulting freedom from sin is summarized in the vision of God's love for humanity reaching its goal in this community of love. Verse 17 applies the indwelling language to the life of the believer. "Just as he is so are we in this world" must refer to the author's application of divine attributes to the believer's life as the basis for both his confidence and his behavior.

It is likely that the distinction between "saying one loves God" and actually loving fellow christians is the Johannine formulation of the common paraenetic distinction between merely saying and actually doing (cp. 1 Jn 3:18). Some scholars suggest that v.21 is the Johannine formulation of the double command of love of God and neighbor (Mk 12:28-34 par) rather than a variant of the single command "love one another" from Jn 13:34. Such a form of the double command might have been part of the synoptic-like Jesus tradition that circulated in the Johannine community. The double form of the injunction appears when the theme of mutual love reappears in 5:2. There it is combined with the earlier formulation about keeping God's commandments.

THE VICTORY OF OUR FAITH.
5:1-5.

> **5** Every one who believes that Jesus is the Christ is a child of God, and every one who loves the parent loves the child. ²By this we know that we love the children of God, when we love God and obey his commandments. ³For this is the love of God, that we keep his commandments. And his commandments are not burdensome. ⁴For whatever is born of God overcomes the world; and this is the victory that overcomes the world, our faith. ⁵Who is it that overcomes the world but he who believes that Jesus is the Son of God?

This section makes the transition between the previous discussion of mutual love and the concluding return to the theme of testimony, which will form an *inclusio* with the opening of 1 Jn. It is sometimes taken as part of the previous discussion. However, two traditional expressions of Johannine belief frame the section as an independent unit.

Verses 1-3 reformulate the previous statements about loving God and keeping his commandment of love. The author has used a variety of formulations to connect "being born from God" and keeping the commandments: he is righteous (2:29); does not sin (3:9, seed of God); loves (4:7). 1 Jn 5:1b is the positive expression of the negative one in 4:20a: "Everyone who loves the one who begets (RSV "the father") loves the one begotten (RSV "child")." The author may be quoting an aphorism or proverb well-known in the community. Compared with 4:20b the continuation in v.2 seems a bit paradoxical, although the author must still be reformulating the previous passage. How can "love for God" be the sign of love for "the children of God"? Rather than emend the text as some scholars do, we would concur with the suggestion of others that the author means us to understand "love God and keep his commandments" as a single expression (cp. 2:3, knowledge of God is keeping his commands; 3:10b, children of God do righteousness; 4:21, love of God and brother). Verse 3 reinforces this interpretation. The variation in v.2, then, is closest to the specification of love in terms of behavior toward the christian in need that 3:17 presented as the practical interpretation of "laying down one's life for the brethren." There is nothing esoteric about love for God or for one's fellow christian in 1 Jn. It is demonstrated in the behavior of christians toward each other. Verse 3b adds the claim that these commands are not burdensome. Some interpreters see this verse—like 4:21—as another allusion to the Johannine tradition of the sayings of Jesus (cp. Mt 11:30). Others see it as derived from the jewish insistence that the Law is not burdensome (cf. Deut 30:11). Whatever its source, this saying could well have been an important part of the community's teaching when it had to define its own interpretation of the commands of God against the hostile claims of jewish teachers.

Verses 4-5 return to another theme of Johannine preaching, the christian's victory over sin or the evil one. 1 Jn 2:12-14 tied together forgiveness of sins; knowing the Father and Jesus and victory over the evil one. "World" here is equivalent to the evil one. It carries the same negative sense that it did in the exhortation not to love the world which followed the previous victory proclamation (2:15). This victory is part of the reality of the believer's life because Jesus as Son of God has already overcome the evil one/ world (Jn 12:31; 16:33). He does not have to reappear as judge and divine warrior to destroy Satan and evil people in order to win the victory that God had been promising his people. Some interpreters associated v.5 with the use of the victory theme against the opponents in 4:4. If the victory is one against false teaching, as that association might suggest, then this verse might be the lead into the next section on testimony. Brown, who ends the previous section with 5:4a, finds a strong polemic in these verses (*Epistles*: 565-67). The opponents have demonstrated that they do not keep God's commandments in their failure to love fellow Christians. Therefore, they cannot sustain any claim to faith or knowledge of God. 1 Jn 5:6 also looks toward what is the traditional testimony by revising it to combat the opponents, and is thus related to 5:5. We have chosen to see 5:5 as an *inclusio* with 5:1 on the basis of its use of a traditional christological confession.

GOD'S TESTIMONY TO HIS SON.
5:6-13.

> [6]This is he who came by water and blood, Jesus Christ, not with the water only but with the water and the blood. [7]And the Spirit is the witness, because the Spirit is the truth. [8]There are three witnesses, the Spirit, the water, and the blood; and these three agree. [9]If we receive the testimony of men, the testimony of God is greater; for this is the testimony of God that he has borne witness to his Son. [10]He who believes in the Son of God has the testimony in himself. He who does not believe God has made him a liar, because he has not believed in the testimony that God has borne to his Son. [11]And this is the testimony, that God gave us eternal life, and this life

is in his Son. [12]He who has the Son has life; he who has not the Son of God has not life.

[13]I write this to you who believe in the name of the Son of God, that you may know that you have eternal life.

This section is dominated by the word "testimony," which appeared in the opening (1:2); was alluded to at 4:14, but has not yet been expanded. Testimony played an important role in the fourth gospel which expressed the encounter between Jesus and the world in forensic metaphors. The world is judged by its response to Jesus and his victory over its ruler. The most important sources for the language of this section are the controversy stories in Jn 5 and 8. (The reference to testimony by the spirit of truth in v.7 may also hark back to Jn 15:26.)

Verse 6 goes beyond the confession of Jesus as Son of God to deal with his death as atonement. This theme is linked with baptismal symbolism. If you turn back to the story of Jesus' baptism in the gospel of John (Jn 1:29-34), you will see that 1 Jn assumes his readers know that version of the story. The gospel narrative has reinterpreted the traditional story so that it is not a baptism at all but John the Baptist's proclamation of Jesus as lamb who takes away the sin of the world (see Perkins: 12-14). That proclamation is part of the testimony the Baptist gives throughout the first chapter and follows what he has just told the jews about his own mission (Jn 1:19-28). You will also notice that the coming of the spirit does not apply as much to Jesus—as in the synoptic versions—as to the Baptist. The latter's vision of the spirit is God's revelation to him that Jesus is his Son. Verse 6 alludes to the baptismal story in such a way as to insist that God's (= the spirit's) testimony to Jesus is not just associated with baptism (and Jesus' bringing the spirit) but with his death. Brown suggests that the opponents linked salvation to the incarnation of the divine son. They read the baptism story as a proclamation of Jesus' pre-existence. However, they rejected the view that salvation and the spirit came with the crucifixion of Jesus (Jn 7:39; Brown: *Epistles*: 595-97).

Verses 7-8 are designed to emphasize the testimony to Jesus' death: it is impossible to separate the testimony of the spirit from water and blood. This verse also reminds the audience of an interpretation of the passion story common in Johannine circles and reflected in Jn 19:34b-35, water and blood flow from the side of the crucified Jesus. Scholars also suggest that the author may be referring beyond the gospel stories of the baptism and death of Jesus to the sacramental life of the community. The fourth gospel shows baptism—spirit (3:5) and participation in the eucharistic celebration of the death of Jesus (6:53) as necessary for a person to receive the eternal life brought by Jesus. Jn 19:35 referred to human testimony about the death of Jesus. In Jn 5:33,36, Jesus refers his opponents to the testimony they had received from the Baptist as human testimony. He says that he has no need of such human testimony, since he has the greater testimony of the Father (5:37f; 8:18) both in the works the Father has given him, i.e. to judge and give life (5:36; 10:25), and in the Father's word, scripture (5:39). The reference to the Baptist's testimony probably led 1 Jn to combine allusion to that story with the language of Jn 5. He insists that although the community does have human testimony, the real witness to Jesus is the Father himself, as he has become known to them through the Son. Verse 10 invokes Jn 8:18, the Father's testimony to Jesus. The failure of Jesus' audience to receive his word (or the Father's testimony) shows their father to be a liar, the devil; were Jesus to accept their views he would be a liar as well (8:44,55). 1 Jn comments that people who will not receive God's testimony to his own Son in fact make God a liar. (A positive formulation of v. 10 appears in Jn 3:33, the person who receives Jesus' testimony about the Father is said to "set his seal on the fact that God is true.")

Verses 11 and 12 give the testimony about the Son as it applies to the christian: God has given eternal life to the one who believes in the Son (cp. Jn 3:15f,36; 17:2f; and especially 5:24,26 discussed in connection with 1 Jn 3:14). In other words, the author is not referring to some new, inner experience of certainty but to the existence of a community of believers who are confident that God's love has been shown in his having given them eternal life through Jesus. That community itself is testimony to the truth of the faith as the author has presented it. Verse 12 repeats the demand that a person believe in order to have life (cp. 1 Jn 2:23; 2 Jn 9).

The conclusion, v. 13, echoes the conclusion of the gospel (20:31). Since the audience is christian, the author reformulates his conclusion slightly so as to insist that they know that they have eternal life. Once again, we are faced with the real crisis behind 1 Jn: peoples' faith in their salvation has been shaken, but not their faith in Jesus as Son of God.

APPENDIX: THE COMMUNITY DEALS WITH SIN. 5:14-21.

> [14]And this is the confidence which we have in him, that if we ask anything according to his will he hears us. [15]And if we know that he hears us in whatever we ask, we know that we have obtained the requests made of him. [16]If any one sees his brother committing what is not a mortal sin, he will ask, and God will give him life for those whose sin is not mortal. There is sin which is mortal; I do not say that one is to pray for that. [17]All wrongdoing is sin, but there is sin which is not mortal.
>
> [18]We know that any one born of God does not sin, but He who was born of God keeps him, and the evil one does not touch him.
>
> [19]We know that we are of God, and the whole world is in the power of the evil one.
>
> [20]And we know that the Son of God has come and has given us understanding, to know him who is true; and we are in him who is true, in his Son Jesus Christ. This is the true God and eternal life. [21]Little children, keep yourselves from idols.

Verse 13 might have seemed a fitting conclusion, but the author has one further set of instructions and one more way of drawing the distinctions between the community and "the world." Perhaps the allusion to confidence in eternal life in v. 13 touched off this final instruction. Like the rest of the work, it is largely traditional material. The section falls into two parts: the community's confident prayer to the Father (vv. 14-17) and the separation of those who serve God from a world under the dominion of Satan (vv. 18-21).

The section is the most direct reflection of community rules that we find in the Johannine writings even though much of the early language of 1 Jn had parallels in essene rules and in Didache. The author begins with the theme of confidence in prayer that is according to the will of God (cp. 1 Jn 3:21f). But he is not dealing with petitionary or intercessory prayer in general. He is referring to formal acts of prayer in the community. Mt 18:15-20 illuminates this passage. It describes legal proceedings to be taken in christian communities to win back a brother who has sinned. There are three elements in the process. First, there are steps to be taken in admonishing and bringing back the brother: private conversation, private conversation with witnesses, and if that fails, public presentation before the community. (The essenes also had detailed procedures for bringing a grievance against a fellow member before the leaders of the community.) You will have noticed, of course, that Matthew places this legislation within the context of Jesus' teaching on forgiveness by having him tell Peter that there is no limit to the number of times an erring brother can be forgiven. Second, someone who refuses to acknowledge the decision of the community assembly is excluded. Members are no longer to associate with him—he becomes as a "tax-collector and sinner." Third, the authority to make such judgments is grounded in two sayings of Jesus: His gift of the power of binding and loosing and his presence at the prayer of the gathered community (2 or 3 were the required number of witnesses). *James* also mentions such community assemblies. Jas 2:1-7 warns against partiality towards the rich in rendering judgment. (Jewish law also contained rules against allowing the social status of litigants be indicated either in their dress or in the way in which they were seated.) Jas 5:16-20 mentions community prayer for the sick, for forgiveness of sinners, and finally the efforts—including prayer—which brothers should make to return a sinner to the community. Thus the connection between confident prayer and winning back the erring member is securely established in early christian community rules. These rules form the context out of which this passage is speaking. The erring brothers in this particular case would be the opponents.

But Matthew shows that there were also limits to what a community could tolerate. Forgiveness can be extended any number of times, but a person who refuses to acknowledge the judgment of the assembly cannot continue to be a member. In 1 Cor 5 Paul demanded exclusion of a notorious sinner. The essenes too had various degrees of exclusion from association with members of the community. A person might be excluded from association with the general membership to be rebuked by the teachers of the community until he repented. But someone who had been in the community over 10 years and lapsed could never return. All members of the sect are to avoid such a person, and are exhorted in general not to enter into relationships or even religious discussions with "those of ill repute" (e.g. 1 QS 7.18-25).

These rules and warnings help us understand the "sin unto death" (RSV "mortal sin") and the language of separation in vv.18-21. Originally, the "sin unto death" was probably the reverse of the belief in Jesus that brings eternal life, that is, denying one's belief in Jesus during persecution. We have already seen what a crucial role slogans about Jesus had come to play in the identity and language of Johannine christians. Those who deny Jesus are excluded from life (1 Jn 2:22f). Oaths of allegiance may have been required during those times. 1 Jn 4:2 suggests an attempt to impose such an oath on the opponents. Note that the language of "listen/not listen" appears in the context of the judicial assembly in Mt 18.

Verses 18-20 use images from Jn 17 to reinforce the separation of christians from outsiders. These metaphors had been an important source of self-identity during the time of persecution. 2 Jn 10-11 show that the author would like to apply a rule of non-association to the opponents such as we find in the various community rules. The warning against idolatry (v.21) may be associated with such rules. In the Old Testament idolatry indicated apostasy from judaism; for the essenes, departure from the teaching of the sect though not necessarily from judaism. In 1 Jn the opponents are christians, not outsiders who would lead a person to deny Jesus altogether. The author has their false teaching in mind when he warns his audience to avoid idols (Brown, *Epistles*: 628-629). The opponents fit the characteristics of those the essenes will not allow to return to the sect if they lapse. They have been members for a long time but have left ("gone out from us," 2:19). They seem to be engaged in encouraging other christians in the Johannine community to follow their lead. When 1 Jn says that there is no prayer for such people essenes will not allow to return to the sect if they lapse. They have been members for a long time but have left ("gone out from us," 2:19). They seem to be engaged in encouraging other christians in the Johannine community to follow their lead. When 1 Jn says that there is no prayer for such people (a reapplication of an earlier rule about apostates during persecution?), he suggests both that they cannot be reconciled with the community and that members should not associate with them even for the purpose of trying to bring them back as they would do for any brother who was in sin. We learn in 2 Jn that they also fit the criterion of Mt 18 in not acknowledging the authority of the elder, the "listen to us" of 4:5. Thus, once again the author identifies his opponents as christians no longer but as those who belong to the world, who are opposed to God.

Some people have found this position extremely harsh

for someone who stresses the centrality of mutual love in the identity of the christian community and in its vision of God. First of all, it is clear that love is never indiscriminate acceptance of a person no matter what. It is defined by specific ways of treating fellow christians, which cross social barriers, like sharing one's goods with the needy. Secondly, although the author's rhetoric implies that the opponents "hate the brethren," he has no specific moral charge against them. But the effect their preaching is having in the community is another matter. He wishes to show that rejecting Jesus' death as atonement for sin strikes at a central manifestation of divine love for humanity. Later gnostics are quite capable of conceiving the love of God in his sending Jesus to redeem those imprisoned in sin and darkness; they might even have argued that the best one can make of the death of the revealer is that it shows up the inherent hostility to the divine which is characteristic of this world, but to suppose that a loving God would tolerate or worse demand the death of his Son is ludicrous. The crisis in the Johannine community seems to have fallen on the pastoral side. Baptism, forgiveness through Jesus' intercession, and atoning death were all ways in which the community saw itself called to a degree of sinlessness and perfection that could give testimony to Jesus and divine love in a hostile world. Their crisis of confidence might even undermine another central insight of the Johannine tradition: Jesus has won the victory over sin and death so that forgiveness, eternal life and friendship with God belong to christians now. They are not contingent on a future judgment. The author has tried to use the Johannine tradition of ethical teaching, its insights about God and confession of Jesus to motivate mutual love and confidence without appeal to burdensome legal rules or strict ascetic purification. Because the author sees that the opponents' position threatens fundamental truths of Johannine christianity, he adopts a rather rigid position toward those responsible for the preaching.

His characterization of the separateness of the community in vv. 18-20 collects metaphors by which Johannine christians had traditionally expressed their unique status over against external hostility. They alone have salvation and life from the true God (v.20). These verses can be best understood as a sustained allusion to Jn 17. Christ keeps christians from sin; from the power of the evil one (v.18; Jn 17:12,15; 1 Jn 3:6). They are not of the world, which is in the power of the evil one (v.19; Jn 17:16; 1 Jn 4:4-6). Jesus' coming has given them true understanding of the Father (v.20; Jn 17:6-8,14,17; 1 Jn 2:12-14,20f). The result of their knowledge is unity with the Father and Jesus (Jn 17:21, 23,26; 1 Jn 3:24; 4:13) and eternal life (17:2f; 1 Jn 1:2; 2:25). Some commentators also suggest that Jesus' refusal to pray for the world (Jn 17:9) is the basis for the refusal to pray for those who have committed the "sin unto death" (v.16c) — a rule that may have come into being during the persecution when christians denied their belief in Jesus rather than be excluded from the synagogue. 1 Jn invokes that rule against the opponents just as he has applied all the other negative imagery from that conflict to them.

Because Johannine language is always in terms of I (Jesus); we or you (pl) and them, and says nothing explicit about the internal organization of christian communities, people tend to interpret its piety as centered on the individual and his or her faith, on experience of the indwelling of Father or Son, and on the individual's love of God or personal sins. 1 Jn has no indication of any such personal piety. On the contrary, the author presupposes community discernment of the true tradition. The language of his paraenesis is directed toward the community of believers, not toward individual experiences of faith. His use of the language of the fourth gospel as community instruction and self-identification probably indicates the way that language was generally understood. Persecution seems to have intensified the images of mutual love and solidarity in opposition to a hostile world. Perhaps it even left Johannine christianity disinclined to develop community structures along the authoritarian lines of the synagogue, since religious leaders and teachers had been the source of persecution. No individual authorities guarantee the tradition.

The author appeals to the testimony of the community as a whole. Tradition is in the common memory and testimony. The traditions of the community were not labored over as texts but spoken aloud and held in memory either as stories of Jesus or as general rules, aphorisms, or short formulae which identified belief in Jesus, community identity, or proper christian conduct. One must belong to the community of those who "know God," "love the brethren" etc. The author of 1 Jn does not give us enough information to tell whether his opponents really preached an individual piety and asceticism as is often suggested. What we can see is his mobilizing all the authority of the community's tradition and past experience, of its language and story, of its paraenesis and rite, to focus an identity, an image of God and salvation, that will confirm the confidence of his audience in the salvation and victory that is theirs as long as they remain in that community of believers.

Two and Three John

LETTERS FROM THE ELDER

The Letter Form

TWO AND THREE JOHN have the length and format of the type of private letters that survive in abundance from the graeco-roman period (see Brown, *Epistles*: 788-95). Letters have four sections:

(1) *Opening*: "from x to y, greetings"

(2) *Health wish*: the opening is often, though not always, followed by wishes for the good health of the addressee; sometimes a report about the sender's health, or an indication of those from whom the sender has had news of the addressee. Sometimes a health wish appears at the end of a letter instead.

(3) *Body*: The writer states whatever business has prompted the letter. The body may conclude with reference to the sender's travel plans, if these have not been the main subject of the letter; or with a recommendation for the person bringing the letter, if the letter as a whole is not one of recommendation. Both occur at the end of 3 Jn.

(4) *Closing*: "farewell." Sometimes the closing includes greetings to other members of the family to which the sender writes or to friends or from people who are with him. Private letters are typically short. They contain only as much information as is necessary to convey the sender's message.

With the exception of Philemon, the Pauline letters are obviously something of an anomaly. They are much longer and devote themselves to instructing the community. But

some of the innovations of the Pauline letter also appear
in 2-3 Jn. The greeting and closing are expanded with bene-
dictions. The health wish is usually replaced by an expression of gratitude for the fidelity to christian faith of the
community to which the author is writing. Naturally, since
he was a travelling missionary, Paul usually has references
to plans to visit the communities in question. 2-3 Jn show
shorter elaborations in these directions but remain within
the length and format of a private letter. Some commentators make a great deal over differences in language and style
between 2-3 Jn and 1 Jn or the fourth gospel (see Brown,
Epistles: 14-32). However, these differences are not so great
that they could not be accounted for by noting that the latter
are intended as formal statements of the tradition, they use
its public language, and were probably read aloud. 2-3 Jn,
on the other hand, represent private style rather than public
exposition.

Author, Addressees, Context

Interpreters disagree about the extent to which 1-3 Jn
may be used to interpret each other. Some treat them all
as phases in the history of a single, worsening conflict.
(Diotrephes turns the table on the elder in 3 Jn.) They see
progress from general admonition against false teachers
(1 Jn), to having them expelled (2 Jn), to being expelled by
them (3 Jn). As will become evident in the exegesis, we do
not favor such a construction. 1-2 Jn seem to be concerned
with the same problem. On our reading of 1 Jn 5:14-21, the
elder's position against associating with false teachers is
the same in both. 3 Jn deals with a different problem.

One of the difficulties in assessing these letters is the lack
of specific details about the sender in 2-3 Jn and the addressee in 2 Jn. The author simply refers to himself as "the
elder." In the pastoral epistles, that term is the title of a
specific office within the community (cf. 1 Tim 5:17), but
there is no indication of such an office in Johannine circles.
The author never appeals either to apostolic authority

or to authority that he holds from the community—unlike the pastoral epistles. Therefore, most scholars assume that "elder" was an honorary title given a well-known christian by communities who honored his teaching but were not formally bound to his authority. This informal authority may be reflected in a letter from 4th century Egypt. A member of a small christian sect writes to ask for aid for a christian who has gone bankrupt and whose children have been taken by creditors. (*Selected Papyri* I #160, Loeb Classical Library; this is the concrete side of the love command!) The addressee is obviously a person of some wealth and influence in the community, since the sender expects that he will be able to help this unfortunate christian out of his difficulties. The name of the addressee on the outside is followed by "elder." We suggest that no ecclesiastical office is involved in this case either. Brown proposes that "presbyter" was a title of office in the Johannine communities for persons who were bearers of the tradition, perhaps a disciple of the Beloved Disciple (*Epistles*: 647-51). This suggestion is based on the author's claim to embody the community testimony and to convict the opponents of error. However, one would prefer to find some appeal to the Beloved Disciple much as one finds Pauline disciples sending letters in the apostle's name (1 & 2 Tim.; Tit.). Therefore, we can only draw the conclusion that "elder" indicates a person of wealth and standing within the larger community. Such usage fits the context of 2-3 Jn and authority in Johannine communities very well.

A second puzzle in the opening of 2 Jn lies in the failure to specify the addressee (see the detailed discussion in Brown, *Epistles*: 651-55). Some scholars have supposed that the expression "elect lady" refers to an individual rather than to a community. "Lady" (or the masculine "lord") frequently appears in the opening of letters from children to parents—or, more generally, where the sender is in a relationship of dependence on the addressee, as in the unusual case when a father addresses his son in that fashion. They propose that "lady" refers to a woman of wealth and influence, probably the person in whose house the local church met. Both the Pauline letters and Acts give examples of christian communities meeting in the homes of such women (e.g. Philm 2; Col 4:15; Acts 12:12; 16:14). The church in a given area seems to have been made up of a number of such smaller groups which gathered in individuals' homes. However, this interpretation founders on the author's use of "children of your elect sister" to refer to christians with him who also send greetings to the community addressed. Another suggestion is that the lack of specific addressee—or at least a region to which the letter is going—shows that 2 Jn is not a letter at all. Rather, they suggest that it was composed on the basis of 1 Jn to be used by travelling missionaries to impose sanctions against false teachers by appealing to the authority of the author of 1 Jn. Copies of 1 Jn may have been circulated with it. We think that 1 Jn itself intends sanctions against false teachers, and, finding no difference in outlook between the two letters, suppose that the author of 1 Jn composed 2 Jn, perhaps as a cover letter for 1 Jn, and directed it to communities besides his own threatened by the preaching of the false teachers.

3 Jn, on the other hand, seems to be concerned with a different problem. Christians who travelled from place to place depended on local communities, house churches, for hospitality and assistance. Not surprisingly, hospitality is frequently mentioned as a key christian virtue (cf. Heb 13:1f, the first example of brotherly love is hospitality; Rom 16:1f; 1 Pet 4:9). These travellers also carried letters and news from one community to another. In 3 Jn, the elder needs to obtain hospitality for his associates after they have been denied it by another group under the influence of a man called Diotrephes. Presumably the two groups are house churches in the same area.

It has almost become customary to assume that Diotrephes was assuming the leadership role of a monarchic bishop known to us from the letters of Ignatius of Antioch, and that the "elder," representing the older charismatic style of leadership, stands opposed to this development of ecclesiastical office (Von Campenhausen: 141; Schnacken-burg: 301). Just as there is no evidence that Diotrephes was associated with the false teachers, there is also no evidence for such a conflict over church order. The Johannine language tradition lacked the type of symbolism to which hierarchical ordering of the community could attach itself. That gap may have inhibited the development of community structures.

Diotrephes probably represents a different reaction to the break-up of the original Johannine *koinonia* than that of the presbyter's opponents. 3 John is not concerned with theological disputes between the presbyter and Diotrephes. Its conclusion lacks the special appeal for *koinonia* that we find in 2 Jn 12. Perhaps, Diotrephes has concluded that the fracturing of the original missionary fellowship means that a Johannine *koinonia* no longer exists. Therefoe, no travelling missionaries, whether from the elder or his opponents, can claim support. Thus, 3 Jn may stand at the beginning of a transition out of the missionary period toward local autonomy for some Johannine churches (see also Dodd, *Epistles*: 1x).

We conclude, then, that 2-3 Jn give us glimpses into the private relationships of Johannine christians. They also show us that the Johannine community was not just a single group but was spread over a region—that around the city of Ephesus. (so Brown, *Epistles*: 102-103). The Johannine writings indicate several different groups: that in which the elder lives; the group or groups to which 2 Jn is addressed; that around Diotrephes, and another (in the same region?) around Gaius. These communities are linked by the travelling of missionaries and others from one to the other and by their common Johannine tradition.

TWO JOHN

AVOID FALSE TEACHERS

Outline

2 JN CAN BE outlined easily following the model of the private letter presented in the previous section:

(1) *Opening*: vv.1-3. Note that the standard short greeting has been expanded with a benediction in v.3.

(2) *Health wish*: Missing. But we find a version of its Pauline equivalent, the thanksgiving for the faith of the addressees in v.4. (Paul usually speaks of giving thanks to God; the elder speaks only of his own satisfaction with the community.)

(3) *Body*: vv.4-11. The author presents the real business of the letter: no dealings with false teachers. Note that he presents his suggestion as a petition (v.5); not as an authoritative command.

(4) *Closing*: vv.12-13. It includes potential travel plans and the greeting from members of the author's community. We have already observed the peculiarity of this letter over against the usual private letter, its lack of detailed address. Perhaps it was intended for more than one group that made up the Johannine church in the area.

GREETING.
1-3.

> The elder to the elect lady and her children, whom I love in the truth, and not only I but also all who know the truth, ²because of the truth which abides in us and will be with us forever:

> ³Grace, mercy, and peace will be with us, from God the Father and from Jesus Christ the Father's Son, in truth and love.

"Elder" is an honorary title, not an ecclesiastical office. It indicates that the person was someone of position and respect within the community. "Elect," a jewish term for the faithful people of God, is often used of christians (e.g. 1 Pet 5:13). Paul often refers to members of his churches as "children" (e.g. 1 Cor 4:14; 2 Cor 6:13; Gal 4:19). "Children" was also a favorite self-designation among Johannine christians. "Beloved" is another common form of address (1 Jn 4:1; cf. 2 Tim 1:2). The author adds "in truth" to his expression of love for the community. Though the phrase could be merely adverbial, "truly," the autho˙ uses "truth" as a catchword for the opening section. He uses "truth" in its full theological import, revelation of the Father in Jesus (Jn 1:8; 2:4 etc.) Johannine christians also apparently referred to themselves as "those who know the Father/God" (see above 1 Jn 2:4). "Those who know the truth" as descriptive of christians in v.1b is a variant of that tradition. Verse 2 makes the same point by using another favorite metaphor "abiding in/with" (cf. Jn 14:16f, with spirit of truth). Once again the author is expressing the Johannine understanding of community as the place in which divine presence is found. The author may have centered the opening around "truth" because he intends to oppose the false teachers.

The benediction of v.3 is typical of christian modifications of the jewish "grace and peace" (as in Gal 6:16; Jud 2) to a three-part "grace, mercy and peace" (e.g. 1 Tim 1:2; 2 Tim 1:2, note that Timothy is "my true child in the faith"; such language about "truth and faith" characterizes later christian writings faced with the problem of diverse christian teaching). Pauline examples show what was probably the usual ending, "from God the Father and Jesus Christ our Lord." 2 Jn 3 in typically Johannine fashion has "Jesus

Christ the Father's Son." The final "in truth and love" is an *inclusio* and leads into the next section—a simpler example of a mode of composition common in 1 Jn. The body of the letter will follow a typically Johannine progression. The author will appeal to the community's tradition of love for one another as command from God before turning to attack the false teaching of the opponents and suggesting measures to be taken against them.

WALK IN LOVE.
4-6.

> [4]I rejoiced greatly to find some of your children following the truth, just as we have been commanded by the Father. [5]And now I beg you, lady, not as though I were writing you a new commandment, but the one we have had from the beginning, that we love one another. [6]And this is love, that we follow his commandments; this is the commandment, as you have heard from the beginning, that you follow love.

We have seen that the *captatio benevolentiae* of v.4 substitutes for the usual health wish after the greeting. It also provided the transition to the body of the letter. As in the opening paraenesis of 1 Jn, "walk in truth" refers to living according to the teaching of the community. It is not clear whether "I have found" refers to an actual visit the elder made to the area, to a visit made to his community by christians from that area, or is simply a literary formalism by which the author can associate himself with those whose faithfulness he praises. Some interpreters think that the expression "some of your children" indicates that the author knows that false teachers have already gained a hearing in the community to which he is writing. We saw in 1 Jn that he habitually insinuates that his opponents "do not love the brethren" even though there is no evidence that their position implied immorality.

The opening of v.5 suggests that the letter is a petition; not a command. Petitionary letters frequently begin by stating the background of the case or of the sender's (or his family's) relationship to the addressee before they get around to the actual request. So here. A condensed summary of the community's paraenesis and characterization of the opponents as "apocalyptic enemies" precedes the actual request in v.10. This two-part thrust is typical of the composition in 1 Jn: first the author states the paraenetic tradition, which sets the identity of the community; then he makes a direct attack on the opponents using the rhetoric of apocalyptic preaching.

Verse 5 introduces what 1 Jn has shown us is the command in Johannine ethical preaching: love one another (1 Jn 3:11,23; 4:7,11f). Also, typically, this teaching is presented as known "from the beginning," i.e. such teaching has been given the audience since they first became christians (1 Jn 2:7-9; the expression also has overtones of being part of the truth revealed in Jesus as in 1 Jn 1:1). 2 Jn 6 reads like a reformulation of 1 Jn 2:3-7. We find the combination of love of God, keeping His commandments, and exhortation about how one is to "walk" which is expressed in more elaborate form in 1 Jn 2:3-7.

BEWARE OF THE DECEIVERS.
7-9.

> [7]For many deceivers have gone out into the world, men who will not acknowledge the coming of Jesus Christ in the flesh; such a one is the deceiver and the antichrist. [8]Look to yourselves, that you may not lose what you have worked for, but may win a full reward. [9]And one who goes ahead and does not abide in the doctrine of Christ does not have God; he who abides in the doctrine has both the Father and the Son.

The author now turns to apocalyptic language to describe the danger posed by the false teachers. His images are familiar from the warnings in 1 Jn 2:18-27 and 4:1-6—the former seems to predominate in the author's allusions. With the exception of the change in tense, v. 7 reads like 4:2. The expression "deceivers" recalls 1 Jn 2:26 and "antichrist" applied to a person who will not confess that "Jesus Christ comes in the flesh," 2:18 and 4:3. We suggested (above on 1 Jn 4:2) that the author has modified a traditional christological formula "Jesus came/comes from the Father" to "in the flesh" as counter to his opponents' rejection of Jesus' death as atonement. But even in this context it remains unclear whether the modified formula would serve as a sufficient confessional test to identify false teachers. "Look to yourselves" (v.8) is common in apocalyptic preaching as a warning against falling victim to the snares that Satan will set up for the elect at the end of the age (Mk 13:5,9 par). Concern about losing/keeping one's reward also comes from apocalyptic preaching as the judgment saying in Mk 9:41 indicates. Paul shows such concerns for his own reward as an apostle when he admonishes his congregation to be faithful to the gospel as he has taught it to them (e.g. Gal 4:11). Within the context of Johannine eschatology, that reward, which could be lost, must refer to eternal life as in 1 Jn 2:25.

Verse 9 has more allusions to 1 Jn 2:22-27. Admonishments to "abide in" usually refer to the Father, Son or spirit; here, abiding in the doctrine of Christ (which probably means "about" Christ) makes it possible for a person to "have" the Father. Reference to the spirit's teaching the community occurs in a similar context in 1 Jn 2:27. 1 Jn 2:24 and 5:12 parallel the positive formulation in this passage. Perhaps, "goes ahead" refers to the people described as "having gone out from us" in 1 Jn 2:19. In any case, the point remains the same one the author has been making all along: no one who is not in unity with the tradition which the Johannine community has had from the beginning can claim to have salvation or to know the Father. This verse might apply not only to people actively spreading the false teaching but also to those who are inclined to listen to them.

NO FELLOWSHIP WITH FALSE TEACHERS.
10-11.

> [10]If any one comes to you and does not bring this doctrine, do not receive him into the house or give him any greeting; [11]for he who greets him shares his wicked work.

The author has finally come to the business of the letter: refuse all hospitality to those who teach a different doctrine; do not even speak with them. We will see in 3 Jn that a recommendation for the bearer can come in this position. The business of this letter makes it a parody almost! 1 Jn 5:14-21 invoked sanctions against the opponents indirectly, and we saw in discussing that passage that exclusion from the community in both essene and early christian rules often included the explicit statement that members were not to associate with such people. Such rules are presumably the basis of the author's request.

members were not to associate with such people. In the technical language of associations, all members of an association share in its fruits, whatever their contribution may be. Verse 11, thus, hints that anyone who greets a false teacher is becoming part of that person's association and will share its fruits, condemnation.

CONCLUSION.
12-13.

> [12]Though I have much to write to you, I would rather not use paper and ink, but I hope to come to see you and talk with you face to face, so that our joy may be complete. [13]The children of your elect sister greet you.

This conclusion is almost identical with 3 Jn 13f, which is one reason that those who are worried by the lack of specific address in this letter think that it may have been based on the content of 1 Jn and the format of 3 Jn. Verse 12 concludes with "that our joy may be complete"—very likely a reference to the opening of 1 Jn 1:4. It is typical of cultures which still rely on oral traditions to a large extent to consider written communication inferior to "face-to-face" encounter. People will apologize for writing or entrust the most important part of a message to the associate who brings the letter. Given the verbal identity between this conclusion and that of 3 Jn—with the exception of 12c—one cannot be sure if the author was actually contemplating a visit to the community in question. He may have been using a literary convention to back up his written exhortation with the suggestion of personal presence.

2 Jn does not offer us any substantively new information about the movement which led to the restatement of the tradition in 1 Jn. It does indicate, however, that Johannine christianity was spread about in several communities which were in frequent communication with each other. Both the author and his opponents might expect a hearing within the churches of the area in question. And, the author considers the threat of their teaching serious enough to seek to have other communities exclude such preachers from all forms of fellowship.

THREE JOHN

HOSPITALITY FOR MISSIONARIES

Outline

3 JOHN PRESENTS us with another facet of the loss of *koinonia* among Johannine Christians, refusal to extend hospitality to traveling missionaries. The author does not warn of the opponents in the earlier two letters, here. Consequently, 3 Jn lacks the appeals to Johannine tradition so striking in 1 and 2 Jn. If there is no group which clearly represents the original Johannine association, then missionaries associated with the elder (or his opponents) could not claim hospitality from other Johannine churches. The body of the letter is more complex than that in 2 Jn, since the author has a twofold purpose. He wishes to secure hospitality for his associates from Gaius, and he seeks to explain why Diotrephes has refused to extend such hospitality.

(1) *Opening*: v.1.
(2) *Health wish*: v.2. Verses 3-4 add the thanksgiving for the faith of the addressee which was characteristic of the christian letter tradition.
(3) *Body*: vv.5-12.
   a) background, the addressee's reputation for hospitality vv.5-8
   b) Diotrephes' lack of hospitality, vv.9-10
   c) recommendation for Demetrius (request for hospitality) vv.11-12
(4) *Closing*: vv.13-15.

Although the opening of 3 Jn is the most secular of all the New Testament letters, the health wish is entirely conventional and there is no benediction. Other features resemble Pauline letter style: the recommendation is expanded with paraenesis (v.11); there is a longish thanksgiving (vv.3f); the author intends to deal with the failure of his earlier letter with a personal visit (v.10). These elements are so common in the Pauline corpus that some scholars have thought 3 Jn might have known Pauline letters. However, as we shall see, the problems mentioned in 3 Jn are so typical of those besetting travelling missionaries as they are illustrated in Paul's remarks about his own problems that one would expect closer analogies to Pauline style and language if actual Pauline letters lay behind the form of 3 Jn. 3 Jn probably represents the more common form of "letter of recommendation" carried by travelling missionaries to help them find hospitality in communities where they were not known. Paul tells the Corinthians that he does not need a letter of recommendation such as his opponents have (2 Cor 3:1f), since his congregation is his letter. The conventions of the secular letter were fairly stable over centuries. It is likely, therefore, that 3 Jn represents the conventional form of the missionary letter of recommendation. This form may have developed in christian circles before the great Pauline epistles (recognized even in their time to be something of a departure, so 2 Cor 10:10?) transformed the genre into a model of apostolic presence and preaching.

GREETING.
1.

> The elder to the Beloved Gaius, whom I love in the truth.

The usual "greeting" or a christian variant like "grace and peace to you" is missing from the opening. "Peace to you" occurs at the end of the letter instead (v.15). The description of the addressee as one "whom I love in truth" is identical with 2 Jn 1a and was probably the author's stock opening. "In truth" may only mean "truly" but it will form an *inclusio* with "walk in truth" at the end of the thanksgiving (v.4), which is typical of the author's style. Gaius was such a common name in antiquity that one cannot identify him with any of the others mentioned in the New Testament. Some people have thought that he must have been a member of the community headed by Diotrephes and liable to follow the latter's lead—hence the letter. However, the presentation of the background suggests that Gaius is unaware of the particulars of Diotrephes' action. Therefore, we assume that Gaius was the leader of another house-church in the same region as that of Diotrephes. It is clear that people from both groups travelled to and from the community in which the elder resides. trephes. Brown, (*Epistles*: 731-32), thinks that Gaius was not the leader of another house-church in the region but simply a wealthy Christian with whom the presbyter's associates had stayed in the emergency created by Diotrephes' refusal of hospitality (vv. 3,6a). The explanation of Diotrephes' behavior may be intended to suggest that Gaius set up his house as a church meeting place. However, if this reconstruction is correct, then the presbyter, himself, is creating new division within the Johannine community. Therefore, we find it more plausible that such meetings already took place at Gaius' home.

HEALTH WISH AND THANKSGIVING. 2-4.

> [2]Beloved, I pray that all may go well with you and that you may be in health; I know that it is well with your soul. [3]For I greatly rejoiced when some of the brethren arrived and testified to the truth of your life, as indeed you do follow the truth. [4]No greater joy can I have than this, to hear that my children follow the truth.

The health wish in v.2 is purely conventional. The RSV
has over-translated the verse which concludes: "and that you
may be healthy as you (lit. your soul) are well." "Soul"
often, as here, does not refer to an entity separate from the
body as the RSV handling of the sentence might suggest,
but simply to the person addressed. All the author is saying
is that he knows things are going well for Gaius (from the
people who have reported about him) and he hopes that they
continue to do so and that Gaius remains in good health.

Thanksgiving for the faith or christian conduct of the
addressee is typical. The author uses the language of
"walking in" (RSV "follow") truth found in 1 Jn 1:6f. This
passage is similar to 2 Jn 4, but note that unlike both 1 and 2
Jn, there is no reference to the love command as such. Both
1 and 2 Jn stress it as part of their polemic against opponents
whose teaching the author wishes to show is false to the
tradition. Lack of such a reference here is another indication that the situation of 3 Jn is not that of 1-2 Jn.

The author has learned about Gaius' way of life from
travelling missionaries. Perhaps they had also brought him
the news about Diotrephes. The "my children" in v.4 has
suggested to some that the elder had been a missionary and
was responsible for Gaius' conversion or even for the
establishment of the church in his area, since Paul uses
"children" to refer to his converts (Phil 2:22; 1 Cor 4:14;
Gal 4:19). However, though he does travel in the region,
the elder never claims responsibility for the conversion of
people there. "Children" was a common s⸍ ⸍designation
among Johannine christians (1 Jn 2:1,12,28; 3:7,18; 4:4;
5:21, 2 Jn 1,4), and the author is probably just using his
normal way of speaking to those whom he exhorts. "My
children" could refer to any christians in a community
which would accept his teaching. We favor this interpretation of the verse, because it also seems that the reference
to joy in it harks back to 1 Jn 1:4 where he has written
testimony to the common tradition "that our joy may
be full."

HOSPITALITY TO MISSIONARIES.
5-8.

> [5]Beloved, it is a loyal thing you do when you render any service to the brethren, especially to strangers, [6]who have testified to your love before the church. You will do well to send them on their journey as befits God's service. [7]For they have set out for his sake and have accepted nothing from the heathen. [8]So we ought to support such men, that we may be fellow workers in the truth.

Praising the hospitality of Gaius as well-known among travelling missionaries, sets the background to the body of the letter. Again notice that although hospitality is spoken of as love in v.6, the author does not invoke the love command as such. It was typical of the early christian mission that the beneficence of a congregation might be praised throughout an entire region. Paul speaks in a similar fashion of his own communities. Hospitality, as this passage points out, meant more than putting such people up. It also involved equipping them with whatever was necessary to continue their work. We have vivid examples of both the importance and the problems of obtaining such aid in the Pauline letters. Rom 15:22-26 tells a congregation to which he has no previous ties that Paul hopes to visit there and that he expects support for his missionary work further west. In 1 Cor 9:1-18, Paul defends both the practice of paying missionaries and his own refusal to take payment. But we learn from 2 Cor 11:8f that churches in Macedonia were contributing to his support while he was in Corinth preaching. Phil 4:14-17 are words of thanks to those christians for generous support not only when Paul was working among them, but also during his imprisonment. Phil 2:25 gives them the same title that 3 Jn 8 gives Gaius, "fellow worker." It seems clear that christians in settled communities were instructed to see themselves as sharing the work of evangelization (and in the Philippian case also the glories of apostolic suffering) by supporting the mission.

Both the synoptic and Pauline traditions understand that obligation as derived from the teaching of Jesus himself (Mt 10:10 par; 1 Cor 9:14; 1 Tim 5:18). 3 Jn 7 insists that the christian mission be entirely self-supporting. The missionaries do not seek patronage or hospitality from pagan countrymen, though the stories in Acts suggest that at least the early missionaries must have done so—perhaps later converting their hosts. It would be usual for a person in a new area to seek out kinsmen, family friends, countrymen, or people of the same trade for assistance. If the christian missionaries are now to avoid receiving such assistance from "the heathen," then such "strangers" (v.3) must be able to count on local christian communities for help. The examples in Rom, 2 Cor and Phil are instructive. In Rom, Paul writes in advance to a community which he did not found in order to secure hospitality for himself and assistance with his future plans. 2 Cor and Phil show that even communities indebted to the apostle's preaching for their faith might treat him in different ways. Some (Corinth) gave him no assistance even when he was present; others (Philippi and others in Macedonia) continued to support Paul's work when he was away from them by sending aid.

Thus, it becomes clear that although hospitality was held up as an ideal the actual realities of life made assistance of that sort, especially in a region where one was looked upon as a "stranger," of crucial importance. The generalization in v.8 "become fellow workers in the truth" may have been a standard part of the appeal for such assistance. Here "truth" does not refer to a specific doctrine or ethical precept but to the whole revelation of God in Jesus (in Pauline terms "the gospel"), which was being spread by the missionaries, "those who have gone out in his name" (RSV "for his sake"). "The name," i.e. Jesus', was a common way of referring to christianity in early missionary parlance (cf. Ac 4:17; 5:41; 1 Pet 4:14,16; Jn 15:21).

DIOTREPHES' INHOSPITALITY.
9-10.

> [9]I have written something to the church; but Diotre-
> phes, who likes to put himself first, does not acknowledge
> my authority. [10]So if I come, I will bring up what he is
> doing, prating against me with evil words. And not
> content with that, he refuses himself to welcome the
> brethren, and also stops those who want to welcome
> them and puts them out of the church.

The Pauline examples provide good analogies for what
is behind Diotrephes' action. The author must have written
to a community centered around Diotrephes (perhaps
meeting in his house) and requested support for some of
his associates just as Paul is doing in Rom. That letter
cannot have been 1 or 2 Jn, since it would have dealt with
hospitality; not false teachers. It was probably a short
letter of recommendation such as we have here in 3 Jn.
Diotrephes both refused to give assistance on his own, and
insisted that no one in his group do so either. Some commentators take "and puts them out of the church" to imply
a formal excommunication against those who welcomed the
missionaries. Perhaps, he simply was refusing to allow
such people to come to meetings at his house.

None of the elaborate conflicts over church order that
have been built on this passage seem well supported. Some
have supposed Diotrephes to have been a monarchic bishop,
who had excommunicated people, perhaps even Gaius and
the elder. He has been held up as an example of a hardening
orthodoxy, which found even the teaching of the elder too
gnosticizing to fit the emerging consensus of faith the bishop
was to defend. Or, alternatively, he has been cast as the
successful gnostic opponent, who can do to the elder and
his associates what the latter had tried to have done to him
in 2 Jn. None of these constructions fits the fact that formal
separation between the two groups does not seem to be

involved. Nor does the author use his anti-opponent rhetoric. (See the discussion of these hypotheses in Brown, *Epistles*: 732-39). Brown suggests that Diotrephes' refusal to receive any travelling missionaries may have been more effective in preserving his community from the views of the opponents than the elder had been, (*Epistles*: 738).

Diotrephes may well have wished to establish his community as independent from those associated with the elder. Again, a passage from Paul may shed light on the situation. Phil 1:15-18 speaks of some people who have taken up preaching Christ out of rivalry. The fact that the apostle is in jail is in some way responsible for their doing so. Notice that unlike the opponents of Phil 3, Paul is not rejecting anything these people are preaching; he will even accept such preaching out of rivalry as long as Christ is preached (v.18). It seems clear, then, that some people have started preaching independently of the Pauline mission in the same area in which the apostle and his associates are working. The facts of the case in 3 Jn may be similar. Diotrephes may have decided to make his community an independent center of activity and to break off association with missionary activities centered in other churches. The RSV translation is a little misleading. Diotrephes does not "reject the authority" of the elder; he refuses to "receive (= welcome) us" (v.9), that is, he has denied hospitality to the elder or to his emissaries.

The elder accuses Diotrephes of "loving to be first." That unattested Greek verb may have been the author's own neologism fashioned on the basis of the adjective "love first place." Such expressions are typical of the rhetoric by which society controlled the ostentation of competitive and ambitious men. (Compare the condemnation of those who "love the first seats" in Mt 23:6 par). The expression has no relationship to any office Diotrephes might or might not have. 3 Jn goes on to claim that Diotrephes is doing evil by bringing false charges against the elder. (The RSV has translated a verb which has a technical meaning of "bring a false charge against" as "prating against"). We may presume that in denying the elder's request, Diotrephes had something to say against him. That would be even more the case if missionary associates of the elder were accustomed to pass through the area and stay with people there. He may even have used some of the "who does he think he is" rhetoric which underlies the "loving to be first" jibe by the elder. But anyone who recalls the bitter charges and countercharges between Paul and his opponents, the "super-apostles" of 2 Cor 10-13, or even the language used by the author against his opponents in 1 Jn, must find this a mild exchange indeed. The author does not even pull out his favorite "hating the brethren"—though you will notice that commentators almost unconsciously do so for him when interpreting 3 Jn, and thus miss the comparatively mild tenor of the letter. Brown notes that while Diotrephes is able to expel people from the church (v. 10), the presbyter does not have such authority over against Diotrephes. However, the elder did recommend similar action against the opponents in 2 Jn 10-11, (*Epistles*: 746-47).

RECOMMENDATION FOR DEMETRIUS.
11-12.

> [11]Beloved, do not imitate evil but imitate good. He who does good is of God; he who does evil has not seen God. [12]Demetrius has testimony from every one, and from the truth itself; I testify to him too, and you know my testimony is true.

Finally, the author comes to the immediate business of the letter, recommending Demetrius to Gaius. He first appeals to Gaius to continue the behavior for which he is known. And—lest there be any doubt as to the authorship of 3 Jn—he does so in language which has the overtones of the "official" speech of the Johannine community. Desirable behavior is "from God"; those who do otherwise "do not know God" (cp. 1 Jn 3:6,10; 4:4,6; 5:9). All the resonances of its expressions about testimony are used here simply to refer to the testimony provided by human recommendations (just as other missionaries had testified to the elder about Gaius, v.3). Presumably Demetrius is not one of the missionaries who had received hospitality from Gaius or a letter of recommendation would not have been required. He might have been previously excluded by Diotrephes and now requires a new base in the region.

CONCLUSION.
13-15.

> [13]I had much to write to you, but I would rather not write with pen and ink; [14]I hope to see you soon, and we will talk together face to face.
> [15]Peace be to you. The friends greet you. Greet the friends, every one of them.

Verses 13-14 are almost identical with 2 Jn 12, though the indication of a visit may not have been purely conventional. The author says that he expects to visit the area (v.10). He may also be using the occasion of 3 Jn to establish a welcome for himself with Gaius and his associates. The greetings to the "friends by name" (RSV "everyone of them") does not necessarily imply that the author has a large following in the area already. "Friend" was another self-designation in the Johannine community. (See Jn 15:14f where the departing Jesus who has commissioned his disciples to represent him in the world, now comes to call them friends.)

In its own way 3 Jn is a reflection of relationships between christians in this small network of communities of "friends." Personal ties of support and communication between churches are crucial to the spread of the mission, since there is no overarching structure of church authorities above the local groups or institution that might coordinate their interactions. It is no surprise to find as we do here that these groups were subject to the strains of interpersonal relations typical of a close-knit society of ambitious individuals. What is remarkable—even encouraging— about the example of these early christians is that a higher loyalty, a sense of responsibility for giving true testimony to the word of God, could be invoked in various ways to help people see the necessity of working through such divisions. At least, that could be the case so long as the divisions were not such that they destroyed the very fabric of true testimony and fellowship, itself—as is the case in 1-2 Jn. We do not know how the story of the elder and Diotrephes turned out. Pauline examples show that reconciliations were possible in instances with a much harsher rhetoric of opposition. It seems to us that the restraint of the author's remarks about Diotrephes, in contrast to what he has to say about the false teachers, is not a sign that the latter has greater ecclesiastical authority or is a successful gnosticizing leader, but is a sign that the author genuinely expects that a reconciliation will be effected. He is not out to alienate or cast off a fellow christian.

INSIGHTS FROM THE
JOHANNINE LETTERS

WHENEVER CHRISTIANS have had to confront challenges to their belief, they have developed new understandings of the essential elements of their tradition. It is clear that the Johannine author has not worked out a doctrine of the relationship between divine and human in Christ as it impinges on salvation. Some people have even found the articulation of atonement theory in Hebrews superior to 1 Jn, since Heb tries to explain the necessity for Jesus' humanity and obedience as an integral part of his having offered the perfect sacrifice for sin. But the focus of the discussion may have been such that the author did not feel compelled to answer that question.

The spotlight on the relationship between Jesus and the Father cast by the fourth gospel always inclines interpreters to look for christology as the issue in Johannine writings. The letters, in fact, back away from the spotlight and speak much more often of God directly than does the gospel. Not because they reject the insights of the gospel—they are too imbued with its insights and language for that!—but because Jesus in his relationship to God is not the issue. The letters make clear that the Johannine church found more in its tradition than Jesus, the revealer. It found a new sense of God, and community. But what has shaken people is apparently a new set of questions about their own salvation. How were people pleasing to God? How did what had happened in Jesus affect their status with Him? How far did forgiveness extend? Did the individual have to achieve a heroic level of purity and ascetic holiness in order to gain eternal life? The author has focused on divine attributes, notably, "God is love" and tried to show how these attributes may be seen to be embodied in the community. Love, sinlessness, justice, perfection all belong to that community because God dwells with it.

We must constantly remember that ancient cities were small places. People all knew each other's business, and each other's conduct much more intimately than we do today. Perhaps in a small town or in the old quarters of Cairo or Jerusalem or in the villages of the Near East, one can gain some sense of what such a face-to-face society is like. The demands made on the christians by the expectation that their mutual love would reflect that of God manifested in Jesus could hardly be a matter of "private" conduct in such a context. Acts of both loving and hating the brethren would become matters of community knowledge even beyond christian circles. Thus, one should not think that a New Testament author's reference to "seeing your brother sin" meant that christians were going around prying into one another's lives. Everyday life in crowded streets—and most life takes place outdoors, in public—and crowded housing provides plenty of opportunity to observe one's brother.

The Johannine insistence that the community "show forth" what it means for God, who is invisible, to be love, perfect, righteous etc. is never presented as the achievement of community organization, as something which any group might achieve. 1 Jn sees the possibility of such relationships as dependent upon a christian "knowing God," that is, knowing that God has "first loved us" and has made perfection and forgiveness available through Jesus to those who belong to the christian community. In some respects, this community had to be uncharacteristic of other types of social association, since it demanded that its members transcend their normal social prejudices. Even their self-designation "friends" contrasts with the ancient view that one's friends were people like oneself in class, education, wealth etc. They claimed, on the other hand, that friendship was established by Jesus for all who believed in him. When we add to all this the strongly traditional character of graeco-roman society, which stressed family, status, hierarchy, competition, we begin to see that "loving one another" could have many ramifications. It was hardly a benign and pious reduction of the ethical teaching of Jesus to a single commandment.

We can also see the demands today that the church somehow be identifiable with the character of God as the one who seeks and saves the poor, the outcast, the captive, those denied human rights or whatever is another way of trying to realize a similar ideal. In our world there is a great contrast between small-scale individualism and private religious life and the large scale of institutions and bureaucracies, all magnified by electronic media. This contrast between our private small worlds and the large, visible media world "where the action is" makes it harder for christian communities to be meaningfully visible in the Johannine sense. I can think, for example, of many fine examples of just the kind of concern for neighbor that the Johannine writings insist show God's presence in the community, right here in my own parish. But many of these examples would not be known to the whole parish, let alone to the larger community in which we live. To try and broadcast them would not only be ludicrous, it would deprive them of the personal, human character which seems so fragile in our world. In the Johannine world, they would be known throughout the community. In our world, people have nothing else to focus on than the large-scale institutional gestures of a religious group and these turn out to be very difficult to endow with the sign value a Johannine understanding of church would seem to demand. 1 Jn would warn us that however we address the problem, we must also remember that human achievements and programs do not create the perfection and salvation about which he speaks; that has come as a gift from God.

1 Jn also faced a crisis of confidence. Christians were uncertain about whether salvation was theirs or not. Once again we have a crisis of confidence that the 20th century has magnified beyond anything the Johannine author might have imagined. Constant war and turmoil are certainly not foreign, but they have more powerful weapons of destruction; the possibility of "peaceful" nuclear accidents; global energy and economic crises painfully analyzed on T.V. every day—all come together to convey the impression that the world is out of control. Secular and religious cults and saviors are all over the media. No one is very confident that our knowledge, our political and legal systems, our economy or any of our traditional values and religions can stem the rising chaos. So, people try the private sphere of self-help, meditation, devotion, anything that promises personal peace, freedom from stress, anxiety or whatever. And all too often this shift means giving up on the ills that beset the larger community. 1 Jn claims that real trust and confidence can only come from God's action toward the world as a whole. One cannot accept the attitude that there is only as much salvation or peace in the world as human beings manage to create for themselves. And, he also will not create confidence by indulging in the kind of doomsday preaching that assures a small group of the elect that this mess is about to end and all will be condemned except themselves. In the Johannine tradition, real confidence is grounded in the insight that Jesus' life and atoning death have broken the stranglehold of evil. And before we reject that idea with "that's easy for them to believe" we should remember how little of what we take for granted in tradition, social support, numbers, those Johannine christians had to nourish their faith.

Since that victory did not magically transform the world, it would have been meaningless without testimony. The Johannine community often seems so small and self-enclosed that we lose sight of its genuine missionary consciousness. We have seen the coming and going of missionaries among communities. Even the opponents who constitute such a danger are indication of a living dialogue of ideas. Testimony must also involve evaluation, since new expressions of faith cannot run counter to the fundamental insights of the tradition about the way in which Jesus shows God's love for humanity. We might also add that christians cannot have confidence in their salvation unless they have a sense that there is something important to say and bear witness to. And it will be in the nature of anything important or true that it will be opposed to things others may be saying. The Johannine example shows the absurdity of a common modern sentiment that every religious statement should be accepted if the person making it is sincere, really believes it. 1 Jn's opponents were sincere christians. 1 Jn does not even accuse them of being in it for the money—a common charge in ancient times as well as modern ones. The best he can do is to interpret their separation as "hating the brethren." Whatever their precise doctrine was, the implications of their preaching cannot be accepted. It seems to have destroyed people's confidence in their salvation, and perhaps, even undermined the vision of the love of God on which the Johannine community sees itself to have been founded. The author can still appeal to the community's own discernment of the tradition as they have learned it from the beginning to counter such preaching and lead them to true insight into what Jesus has accomplished. Christians today, perhaps, first need to understand some of these insights, what really has been handed on from the beginning, before they can figure out how to test the various modern spirits and how to witness the victory of Christ in today's world.

SUGGESTIONS FOR FURTHER READING

COMMENTARIES:

The following commentaries are written with the scholar in mind:

BROWN, R. *The Epistles of John.* (Anchor Bible #30). New York: Doubleday, 1982.

(A thorough, scholarly commentary, which includes a fresh translation of the Johannine letters.)

BULTMANN, R. *The Johannine Epistles.* trans. R.P. O'Hara. Philadelphia: Fortress, 1973 (Ger[2] 1967).

SCHNACKENBURG, R. *Die johannesbriefe.*[4] (HTKNT XIII,3). Freiburg: Herder, 1970.

For the moment the best modern commentary available.

COMMENTARIES AIMED AT THE GENERAL READER:

DODD, C.H. *The Johannine Epistles.* New York: Harper, 1946. (Though without benefit of the newer Qumran and gnostic sources, still has useful suggestions for the general reader.)

HOULDEN, J.L. *A Commentary on the Johannine Epistles.* New York: Harper & Row, 1973.

SOURCE MATERIALS:

You can find the ancient writings referred to in the following:

Dead Sea Scrolls:

GASTER, T. *The Dead Sea Scriptures.*[3] New York: Doubleday / Anchor, 1976.

VERMES, G. *The Dead Sea Scrolls in English.*[2] Baltimore: Penguin, 1975.

Gnostic Writings:

ROBINSON, J.M. *The Nag Hammadi Library in English.* San Francisco: Harper/Leiden: E.J. Brill, 1977.
 (= *NHLE* in the text, followed by the page).

Apostolic Fathers (Barnabas, Didache, Ignatius of Antioch):

LAKE, K. ed. & trans. *The Apostolic Fathers I.* Cambridge & London: Harvard/Loeb Classical Library, 1912 & many reprintings.
STANIFORTH, M. trans. *Early Christian Writings: The Apostolic Fathers.* New York: Penguin Books, 1968.

BOOKS AND ARTICLES:

BOGART,J. *Orthodox and Heretical Perfectionism in the Community.* Missoula: Scholar's Press, 1977.
 (Useful survey of opinions about and background material for perfectionism in 1 Jn.)
BOISMARD, M.E. "The First Epistle of John and the Writings of Qumran." J.H. Charlesworth ed. *John and Qumran.* London: Goeffrey Chapman, 1972, 156-65.
BONNARD, P. "La première épitre de Jean est-elle johannique," *L'Evangile de Jean. Sources. redaction, théologies.* (BETL 44). Gembloux: Duculot, 1977, 301-305.
 (Useful discussion of the question of authorship.)
BROWN, R. *The Community of the Beloved Disciple.* New York: Paulist, 1979.
 (An attempt to sketch out the whole history of the Johannine community; large section on the Johannine epistles.)
_____, *The Gospel According to John I-XII; XIII XXI.* (AncBi #29; 29A). New York: Doubleday, 1966-70.
 (Magisterial work on the fourth gospel. The reader of the letters will find appendices on key Johannine concepts useful.)

CAMPENHAUSEN, H. VON. *Ecclesiastical Authority and Spiritual Power in the Church of the First Three Centuries.* trans. J.A. Baker. Stanford: Stanford, 1969, pp. 12-123.

(Classic study of the development of church office; sees 3 Jn as representative of the conflict between emerging monarchic episcopate and older spiritual authority.)

CONZELMANN, H. "Was von Anfang war." *Neutestamentliche Studien fur Rudolf Bultmann.* (BZNW 21). Berlin: Topelmann, 1954, 194-201.

(On the connection between charism and interpretation of tradition in 1 Jn).

DONFRIED, K. "Ecclesiastical Authority in 2-3 John." *L'Evangile de Jean.* 325-33.

FORESTELL, T. *The Word of the Cross: Salvation as Revelation in the Fourth Gospel.* (AnaBib 57). Rome: Pontifical Biblical Institute Press, 1974.

(Helpful study of non-sacrificial interpretation of the death of Jesus in the Fourth Gospel.)

MALHERBE, A. "The Inhospitality of Diotrephes," *God's Christ and his People.* Fest. N. Dahl. ed. J. Jervell & W. Meeks. Oslo: Univesitet, 1977, 222-32.

————, *Social Aspects of Early Christianity.* Baton Rouge: Louisiana State, 1977, 60-70.

(On travelling and hospitality in early christianity.)

MARTYN, J.L. *History and Theology in the Fourth Gospel.*[2] Nashville: Abingdon, 1979.

(Important study of the relationship between the picture of Jesus in the gospel and the conflict with judaism.)

PERKINS, P. *The Gospel according to John: A Theological Commentary.* Chicago: Franciscan Herald Press, 1978. Oslo: Univesitet, 1977, 222-32. Both of these are contained in:

————, *Social Aspects of Early Christianity.* (second edition. enlarged). Philadelphia: Fortess, 1983.

————, "*Koinonia* in 1 John 1:3-7: The Social Context of Division in the Johannine Letters," *Catholic Biblical Quarterly* 45 (1983) 631-41.

(See the author's commentary for further explanation of the interpretation of the gospel behind its use here.)

VORSTER, W.S. "Heterodoxy in 1 John." *Neotestamentica* 9 (1975), 87-97.
(One of several recent articles warning against jumping into a gnostic interpretation of 1 Jn too quickly.)
WHITACRE, R.A. *Johannine Polemic: The Role of Tradition and Theology.* (SBLDS 67). Chico: Scholars Press, 1982.

(Compares the polemic in the epistles and the gospel.)